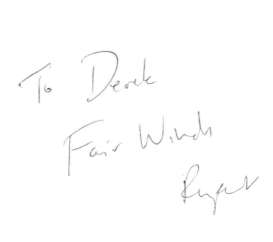

Skippering Kippa

A virgin voyage around Britain

by

Rupert Hugh Emerson

Skippering Kippa is published by Abinger Research Publishing,
Orchard Farmhouse, Wonston, Hazelbury Bryan, Dorset DT10 2EE, UK.

www.kippatravels.com

Copyright © Rupert Hugh Emerson 2008

ISBN 978-0-9560263-0-9

The right of Rupert Hugh Emerson to be identified as the author of this
work has been asserted by him in accordance with the Copyright, Designs
and Patents Act 1988.

A catalogue record of this book is available from the British Library

Thanks

There were many people who helped me throughout the voyage but I would especially like to thank Sarah, my partner, for her perpetual support and constant love. In addition I would like to say a special thank you to Keith and Morris who were both brave beyond the call of duty and Tom, who showed true Scottish grit as well as being tremendous help during my exam. Thank you to my daughters, Monica and Rebecca, for taking part and to Adrian, my brother, and his partner, Andrea, who were both so generous.

A special thank you to Dave and Sue, Kippa's former owners, to Dick and Ange who took Kippa under their wing and Peter, Moira, Ian, Elisabeth and Bill for their hospitality and kindness.

Thanks also to Peter, Joanna, Ann and Juliet, my sister, for always being there for me and to my friends Simon, Katy, Guy, Ashley and Jim for taking part, Martyn and Tony for your help, Christine and Jeff for looking after things at home and everyone at Abbey Sailing Club, particularly Ian, who always had wise words of advice.

I am very grateful to John Rice at Instow, Alex at Lochaber Watersports and the crew of Beluga for their professionalism in times of difficulty.

Thank you to the unsung heroes of our Coastguard, especially the Aberdeen Station, who kept me company and listened out for Kippa in the fog and to the RNLI staff who were always on call and ready to offer advice. And finally, a very special thank you to everyone at Girvan Harbour, especially the lifeboat crew, who did their best for poor Kippa.

Acknowledgements

All the photos were taken by Rupert Hugh Emerson except "Kippa dressed at Topsham" which was taken by Gordon Davidson and "Golden Cap" which was taken by Roger Maude. The name of the book, "Skippering Kippa, a virgin voyage around Britain", was the idea of Tim Austin (formerly of The Times), who kindly proof-read the manuscript.

Rupert Hugh Emerson was a transport researcher and recruitment consultant for twenty years. Tired of working behind a desk, he bought a small yacht and decided that the first voyage should be an attempt to circumnavigate Great Britain. Skippering Kippa is based on the log he wrote during the voyage.

1. Starcross to Teignmouth
Keeping up the spirits

There were several times during the journey that I questioned deeply the wisdom of trying to circumnavigate Britain. None more so than on the first evening aboard.

I was with my younger daughter, the wind was blowing, I was tired and low. Just a short dinghy ride away was a comfortable car and escape. Having Becky with me probably helped because I needed to put on a brave face. I did not want to let her down or perhaps I did not want to let myself down in front of her.

I sensed Becky was nervous but I also thought she was picking up my vibes so if I could wing it, she would be reassured. The best way I could think of maintaining our morale was to play a card game to keep us amused and pass the time. Even though Becky probably realised I was anxious, she went along with my efforts to stay cheerful so that when we went to bed we fell asleep easily after a long, busy day.

It had been a happy afternoon with the kindest, most generous send-off any former owners could have provided. Dave and Sue Rolfe are two of the most genuine people I have ever met. Dave took us across to the mooring with much of our luggage, doing all the donkey work including carrying the dinghy, balancing it on his shoulder as if it weighed nothing. His Sherpa Tensing style of support was so valuable at the start of a voyage that for me loomed like an attempt to climb Everest. Sue was with us in spirit, indeed they gave us a delicious bottle of champagne to celebrate the handover of a yacht that was to become my home.

Starcross on the River Exe is not the easiest place to begin a maritime adventure. It may be a very beautiful spot but to reach a mooring you have to climb a footbridge, negotiate a quayside and then tread precariously down the appropriately named slipway, especially greasy when the tide is going out leaving seaweed on the ramp and smooth round stones at the water's edge. There was also a choppy patch of sea to cross, so an outboard motor was essential to reach the mooring where we were to stay the night on Kippa, our newly purchased yacht.

When we awoke next morning Becky and I were truly on our own. From previous sailing together I knew Becky was a competent crew, would follow directions precisely and hold her nerve, but still my apprehension was intense. This was the moment of truth. Months of planning were now going to be put to the test.

The wind was whistling in the rigging and little waves tickled the hull in the relatively sheltered estuary. Was there too much wind to venture out? I was not sure if I wished for too much or less. Too much would mean an easy decision to abort the trip. Less would mean we were committed to going.

When every possible check had been made, we were ready for the off. Eleven o'clock was the latest I wanted to start and it was now 11.04. Even those four minutes added to the pressure.

Kippa's engine started perfectly and we curled our way along the twisting channel of the Exe behind Dawlish Warren. It did feel better to be on our way at last. A bit better.

Becky showed her awareness of other boats on the move and saved us from early damage when I was raising the sails. The channel by Exmouth was uneven and Becky's face said she was not comfortable. Nor was I, but it was best she stayed on the helm to keep her occupied. Every buoy was a milestone for us that morning and it seemed an age before we could finally turn onto our 225 degrees compass bearing for Teignmouth.

The wind was ideal, just enough to sail along without leaning much; however, the shape of the waves remained less favourable. Soon a town was sighted – could it be Teignmouth? If only. It was Dawlish. Teignmouth was the settlement beyond but at least it was in sight.

Now on the helm while Becky took a rest, I tried to encourage Kippa along at four knots which she would do but only if I pulled on the steering to counteract weather helm which was trying to turn the boat into the wind. If I eased the mainsheet to release the pressure on the mainsail, speed was lost. Telltale ribbons on the foresail told me it was optimally set so I concentrated on steering the right course while Becky read her book and had a doze as we finally overhauled Dawlish.

I was keen to get into Teignmouth around high water, which was at

1 pm. We made it through the channel and up to the pontoon at 1.40 pm. There were no mishaps and we were tied on by 2 pm.

News travels fast and soon after our arrival the Red Arrows made a wonderful, colourful display over the town. We did not see them inscribe KIPPA on the sky but it was fitting enough to have completed our first voyage on a locally important day. To see red, white and blue vapour trails emblazoned above us turned Teignmouth from a seaside backwater into the jewel of the English Riviera.

An extra time pressure on the first day was that we were due to meet our friends Simon, who I have known since early teenage, and his wife, Katy, and their daughters Lizzy and the baby, Esther. After to-ing and fro-ing in Little Kippa, our dinghy, and a few mobile phone calls, we were in touch. Semaphore would have saved at least an hour and some petrol but once we had them on board it felt good. Unfortunately I think they had expected us to provide lunch, which was embarrassing, but we managed with a few scones and they made no complaint. Simon and Katy were typically understanding so we all relaxed. Esther behaved beautifully, Lizzy played with Becky and I sat with exhausted eyes staring out aimlessly until the time came to say goodbye. I was grateful they had detoured on a long journey from London to Cornwall to give their blessing to the little ship and her nervous skipper.

In the evening, Becky and I sought out the little Co-op for supplies to supplement burger and kidney supper. I was exhausted after just five miles of coast and I wondered if I could manage to get as far as Plymouth, let alone turn the corner of Land's End. Teignmouth had reverted to its normal state of being a slightly shabby town where pound shops vied for the most original tat and a larger Co-op made a brash effort to imitate a Tesco. Nevertheless, a certain appeal remained amongst the alleyways, harbourside pubs and a fine row of Victorian guesthouses.

We were moored on a convenient pontoon parallel to a sandy spit, opposite homes where unselfconscious owners sat in their verandas and patios revelling in their little paradise of seaside retreat. On the other side of the estuary it was prettier. Teignmouth has its industrial dockside with large coasters loading from the quay but, on the south side of the River Teign, myriad little boats were neatly moored on a sandbank for the artist to capture on a wide canvas. The bridge that spanned the river was not arched like a Roman antiquity but it gave the view character despite its boxy shape. Beyond the sandbank, which is called The Salty, the houses of Shaldon exuded Devonshire charm.

We did not even consider using the bridge to reach the other side. We could row across in Little Kippa and we had a reason to do this, a chandlery. Unfortunately it was not well stocked for the yachtsman, the friendly owners happy to cater for a variety of other local markets, giving the marine business only a passing nod.

We took Kippa up to the old town quay at high water and the harbourmaster helped us fill up with water from his hose. Becky and I then ventured out of harbour in Kippa but had no intention of going far with the weather looking changeable and a strong wind blowing. We practised the drill "man overboard" until ominous clouds began to scud across.

Then over the hill came a massive black cloud which let loose torrential rain. We struggled onto a pontoon, dancing alongside a large motorboat also trying to get on. As I stepped off Kippa I trod in an inch of water with buckets more crashing down as the sea fizzed and hissed, massive droplets bouncing off the water and splitting into a mist. I just avoided aquaplaning across the planks, got Kippa tied up and took cover.

When the storm had passed, Becky and I explored Teignmouth further, found a lot of what was not available in the chandlery and crossed off half our list. We had a quick shower in the basement of the seafront café, an oversized building that must have appeared in the Fifties at a time of American influenced modernity, when being painted white meant all other architectural criteria could be shortcut. When the drawings were presented to the town council one can imagine the artist's impression included a chrome-plated Chrysler, strutting women in stilettos and Terylene-suited men.

In the late afternoon our neighbours on Blue Horizon, a motor cruiser that had the air of a palace that had seen headier days, kindly invited us aboard. Inside it was like a vast conservatory. It was warm and the people were fun and convivial. There was alcohol on board and the bonhomie of adults letting life's pressures go, carefree like teenagers. You could not help finding a large smile breaking out across the face as you joined in with the party animals, the men trying to hang on to reality, the ladies not. We shared fish and chips and were able to contribute the excellent champagne from the Rolfes to the festivities. The incongruous combination went down extremely well and we returned to Kippa in good spirits.

On our third day we put the dinghy into the harbourmaster's store, picked up the car and collected Camping Gaz.

2. Teignmouth to Brixham

Key trouble

Becky flew back to Spain and on Sunday 27th August I returned to Teignmouth with my girlfriend, Sarah, and her daughter, Joanna. Here was a chance to be dropped off at one port and picked up at the next. A rare luxury. Unknown, as it turned out.

We picked up the dinghy from the store and had lunch together on board. After the meal, I dropped Sarah and Joanna ashore and then Captain David Platt, the harbourmaster, guided me out as the harbour ebbed. Kippa and I followed his launch through the channel and then I tried to thank him for his kindness but was unable to communicate across the water so just gave him a wave.

After struggling with ropes we finally got going with one reef in the mainsail. Kippa sailed swiftly out to the Ore Stone and with Tor Bay looking exposed I reduced the mailsail further with a second reef. Sure enough it was windier but it was comfortable and, with half the jib furled, Kippa shot along on a close reach with the wind coming over the bow, reaching a speed of 6.1 knots over the ground, according to the GPS (Global Positioning System).

After struggling to take sails down, I got Kippa into Brixham Marina and moored beside a charming set of people in a Westerly Centaur from the River Exe. Throughout my voyage I found the owners of Centaurs to be particularly friendly. They love their sailing, adore their boats, treating them more proudly than people with much fancier vessels. All Westerly owners I met were friendly but the people who own the model called the Centaur are a special breed, rather like Morris Minor enthusiasts. Their boats may not be the most up to date but they are tough, easy to maintain and were well designed for their day.

Very pleased with myself for achieving my first solo passage without mishap, I now wondered where Sarah and Joanna might be. Browsing the shops in Brixham? No. I called them on the mobile. They were still in Teignmouth. The car keys were lost. Did I have them? I looked in my pocket. Er. Yes.

So I had to head down to the bus station, pick up the number 12 to Paignton and then take the train. There were no direct services so I changed at Newton Abbot, grabbed a lasagne and a milkshake and finally got to Teignmouth. I apologised because it was really my fault, not Sarah's, but she apologised for not realising too which made me feel a bit less of an idiot. We made our way to Dartmouth where I had rented a flat on the Kingswear side, recognising that Sarah and Joanna were not keen to live aboard. We passed several wonderful evenings in the flat overlooking the River Dart through french windows, which opened out onto a balcony that reminded us of Provence.

There was a downside to our stay. Returning from a quiet afternoon at a National Trust property we got out of Sarah's car to be confronted by a Typhoon military jet doing tricks. It dropped almost on top of us and then blasted its engines in imitation of a Saturn V rocket, making such a horrendous noise that it damaged my hearing. The pain was excruciating at the time but subsided after a few days though the tinnitus lasted months. A year later, my left ear has reasonable hearing and the right ear is dull.

The next trip out in Kippa was on the Tuesday in a force five. Sarah was keen to experience a sail. Joanna was keen to remain on shore. The harbour entrance was choppy and the best we could do was to motor out into Tor Bay, dodging a lifeboat on its way to pick up a jet skier. We got the jib unfurled, turned off the engine and Sarah began to enjoy herself as we sailed back in through the bumpy waves to Joanna who was waiting at the pontoon to take our ropes, glad to see us back safely. Later that afternoon Dave Rolfe very kindly connected up my newly purchased chartplotter to the VHF radio and then he and Sue joined us for a most enjoyable dinner in the restaurant by the marina.

3. Brixham to Dartmouth

Going solo

On 1st September, Sarah and Joanna had to go home so they took me back to Brixham. It was a very sad farewell. From Kippa I watched as they returned to their car and saw Sarah checking up on the lifeboat. She sensed the dangers now that she had been to sea in Kippa and I could feel her concern very strongly.

I made careful preparations that took until 3.30 pm when really I should have left at 2 pm to optimise the tide. I had Salcombe in mind but was aware that Dartmouth would be the likely destination. I motored Kippa out of the harbour and put the sails up. I tried out the autopilot but found it unreliable and settled down at the helm. I felt eyes were on Kippa as we left harbour but once she turned the point we were on our own except for one other yacht. It turned out to be a comfortable and pleasant passage but I felt the pangs of loneliness as I looked up at the coastline where Sarah and I had been walking together, picking blackberries, wandering through fields while Joanna explored ahead of us.

When we came into the estuary of the River Dart I tried to call the marina but had no luck so I called the harbourmaster and requested a town quay berth. I returned to the flat, which still had two nights left on the rental period, and the following morning moved Kippa onto a pontoon outside the yacht club. There the crew of a traditional motor-sailor, also from the River Exe, made me very welcome.

With strong winds outside harbour I decided to do some practice, learn to use the chartplotter, check the autopilot and attempt the procedure of drying out on the twin keels while the tide was out.

Kippa and I sailed up the River Dart to Dittisham, where I picked out a spot on the mudbank and prepared the kedge anchor. Unfortunately Kippa grounded too soon and I was able only partially to correct the situation by pulling on the anchor. Even in this sheltered spot the wind was quite strong.

I made the best of a bad job by knocking up a good meal of spaghetti, mushrooms, fennel and garlic so that even if fellow sailors did not admire my seamanship, they might not think badly of my culinary efforts at the galley.

4. Dartmouth to Salcombe

Conquering Start Point

I cast off at 4.30 in the morning with ropes still untidy. Relying too much on the chartplotter, I made my way with Kippa to the entrance. It was encouraging to find two other yachts coming out with us, so my tidal calculations cannot have been too far wrong. I soon realised that I needed to prepare better for night sailing as I lost time during the first hour getting the tangle created during the night sorted out. We set off very conservatively with two reefs and made slow to steady progress heading more east of south than I would have liked owing to the direction of the wind. I was keen to clear the Skerries Bank safely and waited a long time before tacking. I shook out a reef soon after sunrise and tacked. However, we did not have sufficient speed to be able to clear Start Point on the new heading. I tacked again to clear out from the coast. Once I was certain we would clear Start Point and not go too close to the overfalls I tacked again. I vividly recalled how Monica and Becky and I had been here a year before with my friend Keith Ringsell and all of us were sick except Keith and we were forced to turn tail and return to Dartmouth. I was determined to beat Start Point this time.

It took several hours of beating against the wind before Start Point was close. The tide was still with us and I knew Kippa could make it. As we passed the lighthouse I cursed the seabed which is so full of devilry, a necessary release of my wrath that had been festering since the battering this sea had given in the past. I felt much better for conquering this beautiful headland.

Now Kippa and I were heading for Prawle Point but unfortunately the wind was easing and the tide was slackening. She was making less than three knots through the water and still having to tack so when the tide turned we were in bother. I knew if we tacked out again into open water we might never reach Salcombe on this tide so I put the motor on. The wind died and even with full sail and motor Kippa struggled to make headway. I felt it necessary to let the coastguard know that my earlier trip report was going to be very inaccurate, but having communicated with them in the past on channel 67, I discovered that by this stage along the coast they listened only on channel 16. However, I did get hold of the harbourmaster at Salcombe.

When we got close to the entrance the wind began to strengthen as it funnelled between the cliffs. I had taken down the jib earlier when the wind had given up yet now I could sail in I wondered if there were by-laws about sailing up the channel. I knew Salcombe had strict rules and thought perhaps I would avoid any risk of getting into trouble, even though only in major ports like Portsmouth are they normally concerned about sailing in a ship channel.

I radioed to ask for a mooring and was left to bob about at the Marine Hotel for a long time before a harbourmaster directed me to a sheltered pontoon in the pool up-river called "The Bag". The elation of completing the passage was sending enough adrenalin round my tired body that I found the energy to pump up the dinghy so that I could get to the shops before the end of the day. I finally stepped ashore at 4 pm after almost 12 hours on the go. I sought out the yacht club and found it open but deserted inside. Locals were polite but not friendly, making me feel very much the outsider. From the terrace outside, the club commands fine views which I took in before returning to the village to peruse an interesting if expensive delicatessen. I checked out a busy little café which provided simple sustenance in a fun family environment. I avoided the shops selling sailing gear – the stock was more about pose than practicality.

Once Kippa was floating again on the rising tide I returned to Dartmouth. I cleared out my things from the rented flat and went to bed on Kippa. During the night I was bothered by light through a porthole so I shoved some ropes over a towel to cover it up. In the morning I regretted the tangle I had created.

5. Salcombe to Newton Ferrers
Family album

In the early days of my voyage, I had support from several people such as Adrian, my brother. He knew I needed a base in the South West and just gave me a key to his house. His partner, Andrea, backed him up and made me feel that what Adrian offered was what she wanted too. The fact that they both came sailing on Kippa and shared the experience meant a lot. Naturally I wanted to give them a fun day out. Equally naturally, the first time they came on board was a disaster.

I had wanted to make Kingsbridge a port of call and had planned to take Kippa up the estuary on the high tide. However, with very marginal tidal depth predicted, I decided not to risk it and instead arranged to meet Adrian and Andrea in the dinghy. I had a fun ride up the estuary from Salcombe, filling up with petrol on the way, with a force five wind following me. The waves built up and it became as good as power boating.

We met up in the centre of Kingsbridge and at the quayside we put their gear into the dinghy. We set off together but quickly it became obvious that the trip was not going to be any fun for the passengers. The tide had turned so now the wind and tide were kicking up the waves. Adrian and Andrea were very brave but it felt foolhardy to risk the valuable Riverford Organic produce they had brought for lunch so I took them back to the Kingsbridge Quay, unloaded and agreed to meet them at Salcombe instead. They would drive round while I motored down with the dinghy. I struggled back, employing different speeds and angles to the waves as it grew increasingly unpleasant. I tried to keep in the lee of the trees but equally wanted to avoid a rock or mudbank. It was guesswork without a chart but I made it back to Kippa. I decided that Adrian and Andrea might prefer a water taxi to the dinghy in these conditions so I called up the taxi and asked the driver to bring them across as soon as he had found them. After half an hour I called again and it was obvious that the lad running the service had not bothered to look properly. However, Adrian heard me calling their radio and quickly went into the harbourmaster's office to make contact.

Eventually they were on board but by now the weather had turned from miserable to awful. We cheerfully ate a super lunch but afterwards agreed to return to dry land. We drove to Adrian's house in Plymouth, via a quick drink at Modbury. Adrian knocked up some great soufflé omelettes in the company of Nick, his son, and Roxy the dog and we had a happy, comfortable evening.

With perfect weather predicted I dashed back to Totnes by train, then bus to Kingsbridge and then another bus to Salcombe. Kippa was filled with diesel and water, a can was filled with petrol while we did our best to avoid a crew shooting an Agatha Christie film. Kippa and I then headed off from Salcombe with full sail. After shaking out a temporary reef put in before Bigbury Bay we passed Burgh Island, which has mixed memories for me. My mother loved Bantham, regularly walking there with her dog, but it was also the time when Gaga, my mother's mother, was stuck in a old people's home. Gaga had been an enormous influence on the family, bringing joy and laughter, love and understanding. A happier memory of Bantham was when Sarah, Joanna, Monica, Rebecca and I had been there together, Sarah and Joanna revelling in the sea life, the rest of us playing on the sand.

Happy memories were recalled again as I sought the River Erme, a hidden little river. I was tempted to revisit the anchorage which Keith, Monica, Becky and I had visited. Becky had loved rowing the dinghy that day. She is an explorer and yearns for the freedom of her own craft.

Kippa and I continued towards Newton Ferrers, which is tucked behind a headland, nestling beside the small steep sided valley of the River Yealm. The entrance was straightforward, as I followed the instructions of the almanac, and we took up a place on a visitor's pontoon. I pumped up Little Kippa, the dinghy, and rowed up a tributary in the evening light, making the most of the high tide to carry me past the pretty waterside cottages.

I landed and walked up through fragrant climbing roses to the village post office which I found was imaginatively stocked with organic produce, gifts and essentials. The locals were friendly but it was time to get back to the boat before the tide flowed out. I met Anne and Ewan in Annie-M, a Southerly lift-keel yacht, on the pontoon and they gave me useful advice about safety equipment, which I later followed.

6. Newton Ferrers to Plymouth
Signs of the 70s

I was sorry to leave Newton Ferrers and its partner village, Noss Mayo, both cheerful, picturesque places that I would have liked to explore by dinghy and foot for days, but I needed to get to Plymouth for Saturday to meet Adrian and Florence, his daughter.

Kippa and I got across the River Yealm bar with Little Kippa towed behind and found a strong south easterly building up an awkward sea. The dinghy kept chasing the yacht, climbing a wave and then bumping into the stern. No matter what I tried I could not settle the situation. I tried different lengths on the tow rope. I tried making Kippa go faster or slower but it made no difference. I even tried sailing at different angles to the wind. The experience of being bumped from behind continuously is unnerving and put me off towing the dinghy for months until I regained confidence by using two painters to pull the dinghy and then balancing the movement by adjusting the length of the tow ropes. I had more success when I could set the dinghy to follow at different angles and positions according to the sea state, though perhaps I never met quite the same wind and wave conditions while towing the dinghy as on that day off the Devonshire coast.

I found Plymouth to be a large and complex harbour where my navigation had to be followed with care to avoid vessels of varying size, speed and importance. The warships and the possibility of encountering a submarine were the main worries. The strong wind encouraged me to seek shelter up-river at Torpoint Marina; however, the shallow entrance channel was exposed to the east so we pressed on up the River Tamar to take up a free mooring at Saltash. I learnt why it was free during the next couple of days.

On arrival at the quayside I was met by a man called Marcus who had a wooden Penzance lugger. It was one of those situations where I would have coped on my own but, being an experienced sailor and with a strong spring tide running, Marcus thought it would be helpful to give instructions. This meant adapting my strategy to fit in with him. Despite a bit of a muddle we tied up safely, though the wind did seem to be funnelling under the Tamar Bridge. The situation deteriorated when a Tamarisk 29, an old, heavy, tired wooden boat, drew up alongside and squeezed poor Kippa against the wall.

I survived the night but found Kippa surrounded in the morning by detritus washed down with the exceptionally high tide. The rubbish from 30 years ago had been picked up and carried down, giving an insight into how we lived in the 1970s.

On the same pontoon was a third old wooden boat and I realised then that this was a little corner for live-aboards who had no job and very little money. Their boats were their homes and the wooden interiors were used to adapt to personal preferences. Tea making was at the hearth and objects were strategically placed to make regular brew-ups easy. Cats or dogs were popular, either to keep out rats or humans. Chatting to the owner of the third boat, I sensed that solitary existence had become a kind of survival, while the reason for living was to plan for a challenging voyage; in his case he dreamed of reaching Spain.

I did not feel like one of them, still being the office boy on a jaunt, and I was not sure I envied their freedom, but I did realise that if I did not shave I would soon look like them.

Before starting the engine, I had to clear away the mess of children's toys, vegetation and assorted plastic objects and then I needed to manoeuvre Kippa around to be in position for when Adrian and Florence arrived. When they did step aboard, the unpleasant easterly became a boon as we broad reached, with the wind over the shoulder, up the River Tamar with Adrian enjoying steering. Beyond Weir Quay we anchored but, with the stream running exceptionally fast, it was not wise to get down into the dinghy. We made our way back to Saltash where I dropped my passengers off, then carried on down the Hamoaze, a wide expanse of water where warships are repaired. The tide turned and Kippa found herself tacking uselessly. With motor and full sail we still struggled and it seemed to be hours before we finally made it into Mayflower Marina. A concerned voice from marina control asked if I intended to sail onto the pontoon but I assured them I had had to sail in because of the tide and would now take down sail. They offered me a very short berth which I declined, ending up on a long outer pontoon with the fancy yachts and gin palaces.

Sunday was warm. Adrian and Andrea kindly invited me up to "The Shack", their beach house on the hill above Whitesand Bay for a great barbecue with family and friends.

Afterwards I stocked up the boat but the weather had turned foggy and uninviting so I crossed over to Southdown Marina on the Cornish side of the Tamar. The place was a mess of old pontoons and run-down buildings, one of which served as an office. The owner was helpful and the location rural but the potential to make this an attractive marina had been missed.

7. Plymouth to Fowey

Sea legless

It was Friday 22nd September before Kippa and I set off again, having stayed in harbour while the tail of Hurricane Gordon passed. We slipped out of Southdown Marina, which had almost closed down completely, and made our way up to Torpoint Marina. They refused visitors so it was a brief stop to pick up Andrea. We made our way upstream and turned into the River Lynher in beautiful sailing conditions. At the well known Dandy Hole anchorage we stopped to admire the railway bridge at St Germans. In the distance the arches fell softly out of trees and crossed the water like a Capability Brown-designed folly, before disappearing into a hill on the other side. The pale tones, the lapping water, an old ketch and the ancient oaks created a divine scene. Time was against us so we scooted back to Torpoint to brave the unpleasantness of the marina again. In the evening I dropped anchor by Cremyll, which is across the Hamoaze from Plymouth, where the water's edge is mostly wooded and habitation is limited to a couple of mansions with boathouses by the shore.

On the Saturday Kippa and I set out for Fowey. We sailed out of the harbour, avoiding warships and submarines exercising, and pushed out into a moderate to rough sea around Rame Head. A mixture of boredom, apprehension of a long passage without safe haven and attempting to use the autopilot brought on seasickness. The wind was from a favourable direction creating a broad reach but I could not deal with the shape of the sea. Gradually my strength was sapped and my endurance tested. By the time I had been seasick five times I was really struggling to steer a straight course. I was beginning to wonder if I could make it to Fowey or would have to call for help.

I decided to call up another yacht on the radio. It was a larger boat sailing closer inland and it replied to my call. The skipper understood I was struggling and immediately came up to a close reach to intercept us. When he came alongside I could see by his white beard and complete control of his yacht that he was experienced and wise. He called over to me but we could not hear each other. As he passed he called on the radio and gave me a bearing and distance to Fowey. He treated me with real kindness without making me feel a fool and gave my morale a tremendous lift. Kippa and I followed him as best we could and when he turned into Fowey he called me on the radio to say he would be out of range but that he would be looking out for us when we came into the harbour. He gave me hope and something to strive for.

I struggled on and managed to get Kippa round the final headland and into the river. I called him up to say thanks and he simply told me I would like Fowey, without mentioning my predicament or his unselfishness for staying in touch and guiding me in. I tried not to bother people during my adventures but I was learning that at sea people are usually happy to help if asked. It is a camaraderie lost amongst motorists in these days of mobile phones and fast breakdown services.

When I reached Fowey I was exhausted but not quite shattered, thanks to the support along the way. I moored next to a much larger yacht and discovered that most of the crew had been seasick on the same journey, including the skipper. I felt sorry for them but I felt better myself. Perhaps the sea conditions had been difficult after all and it was not just me.

The next day I was still wobbly so I went exploring. There is a good path along the east side of the river from Mixtow Pill to Polruan. The views from the hill are lovely and the tiny church just up from the ferry is comfy and homely. I crossed the river in the ferry boat but was too late for Sunday lunch everywhere I went in Fowey, so I ended up with fish and chips.

In the evening I motored Kippa up-river using the chartplotter extensively. I turned off to explore the Lerryn, a peaceful tributary with woods spreading out over the water. I chose to lay Kippa on the mud, not sure how best to anchor and dry out. I motored round to find an area with similar depth and then dropped the small mud anchor. Kippa ended up tilted a little but I could not see how to avoid it, short of tying to a tree and then backing off and anchoring. A couple of small dinghies with fishermen motored up-river during the evening and then Kippa and I were completely alone apart from the sound of birds.

There was not a sign of humans. Nature was in charge and I absorbed the atmosphere.

I was now appreciating my choice of a yacht with two keels which was making it possible to sit on the river bottom when the tide goes out. I had seriously considered a traditional yacht with a long keel, such as a Nicholson 26, because they sail well in a difficult sea but decided that I wanted to visit small tidal harbours. I did also consider a lift keel boat but at my budget there was not a model I felt would sail well and be trouble free. I certainly did not fancy the idea of being in a yacht with the keel up when it should be down (or vice versa) as can happen with a lifting keel. A strong twin keel makes it possible to be adventurous – and that evening I certainly felt so.

8. Fowey to Falmouth
Regaining confidence

Next day there was fog. It cloaked the steep valley sides and hid the shape of the river. With it being a completely still morning, I figured it might be land fog and that if I ventured out I might find clear skies. Kippa lifted off the mud and we caught the top of the tide, motored gingerly down-river, following the same curves we had explored the evening before. Things looked different in the pale gloom but the chart-plotter confirmed our position. We slid past the houses of Fowey, which vaguely showed. There was little activity on shore but there was a boat or two on the move.

By the time we were out at sea the fog was lifting. The sea was reasonably calm now and a gentle breeze was beginning. The coastline was mainly green pastures with rocky outcrops, with just the occasional building of interest. The clarity improved when we were out into St Austell Bay and I could now see Par, with its chimneys, and perhaps even make out Charlestown, a harbour famous for historic boats.

I was tempted by Mevagissey, although the wind was increasing and Kippa was making good progress, so we continued on.

Gorran Haven appeared and I had two potential havens now. We were tacking into the south westerly wind, heading out to sea at first and then turning towards the coast, carefully avoiding rocky patches.

When in a clear safe spot, I hove-to and dug out lunch as a few drops of rain fell. The wind increased and I took in a reef in the lee of a cliff and beach just before Dodman. Now inshore I decided to pass Dodman Point close up, knowing the wind would carry us away from the edge if gear were to break. I was keen to be near enough in to avoid the overfalls so I tacked Kippa right up to the land and enjoyed the adrenalin of a late tack away from jagged rocks.

Happy with my sail plan, Kippa skipped along as the wind

strengthened out of the lee of land and into Veryan Bay. The sea became a bit choppy with a force five but it was still comfortable. The wind was veering west and we could sail across the bay without tacking if I kept Kippa close on the wind.

I beared Kippa away from the wind as we approached Gerrans Bay to avoid "The Bizzies" overfalls, seeing no inside passage to avoid them. The tide became stronger now that we were further out to sea and once into smoother water we kept up to windward to close in on Falmouth.

Encouraged by seeing other yachts I pressed Kippa on as fast as I could, taking out the reef when the wind slackened. When we came into Falmouth Bay I was very surprised to see a grand cruise liner anchored in a corner. We had to beat against the wind but this gave me an excuse to get almost underneath the towering Star Princess and watch as passengers stepped out into launches to be ferried over to the town. Once inside the harbour entrance, we turned in to approach the visitors' yacht haven, lining up the clocktower as recommended. It had been a fine day's sailing, never boring, with snacks and fruit to keep me going. I had taken a Travelcalm tablet and did not feel drowsy. With a settled tummy I was in good form to enjoy a meal expertly served at the Warehouse Bistro in the oldest part of the harbour.

The next couple of days I spent in Falmouth. I visited the maritime museum and had fun with their remote control boats. I also found the rooms that had been created below sea level gave a fascinating fish eye's view of the marine environment between low and high tide.

9. The Fal and Truro Rivers
VIPs on board

It was coming to the time of year to decide where to leave Kippa for the winter so we went up to Penryn and I explored the boatyards. Afterwards Kippa and I sailed down to Falmouth and made our way out into the Carrick Roads, a wide expanse of deep water. The wind started howling in the rigging and the rain came down hard so we pulled into the shelter of Mylor, a pretty village on the western shore. On 28th September, the wind had dropped so we had to motor up the Fal. It was warm and dry and the trees were beginning to show their autumn colours. We followed the tortuous but well marked channel into the Truro River to take the last of the tide up to the city of Truro. The harbour office staff were very pleasant and it proved to be a convenient spot with a portaloo and shower on the tiny quay.

I spent a couple of days in Cornwall's capital, visiting the cathedral and then walking to Malpas across the fields above the ria. It was as I descended the hill to the village of St Clement that I came upon a most enchanting view of the lichen-covered church tower nestling amongst trees. At the foot of the path I stopped at a cottage to buy some home-grown produce and ate a tomato and apple on the spot before entering the sweetly proportioned church with its fine stained glass. Before continuing, I studied the labelled plants in the churchyard, which was being managed for wildlife.

The next day Adrian and Andrea came aboard again. The sky was full of stormy clouds but we set off in hope. We got stuck just three metres from the quay. After five minutes and very close to high water we floated off. We quickly dropped down river through the tidal barrier, past a recycling tip and a boatyard lifting yachts out for the winter.

At Malpas we set full sail, then wasted time having a look up a creek to see if we could get a glimpse of St Clement before continuing down

21

to the Fal. The wind was fluky in the lee of the big trees and hills and we made slow progress past the Smugglers Cottage. There was a burst of rain and then the sun broke through temporarily. We passed King Harry's Ferry and came to Turnaware Point. South of us stretched the Carrick Roads, looking forbidding. The options now were either carry on to Mylor or try and get into the quay at the Pandora Inn. Returning up-river did not enter my head until later. With the tide flowing out and a southerly wind blowing into the estuary, the sea was uncomfortable. I put in two reefs and asked the crew how they were. They assured me they were fine, but I should have realised that a change of plan was needed. We began tacking out into the open water. I had been sharing the steering but now it was obvious that I had to remain on the helm if we were to progress windward. Time was marching on and the tide was passing the stage where there would be enough water to get to the Pandora Inn so now we were committed to progressing to Mylor. We could see the harbour in the distance and it was tantalisingly close but it proved a struggle to get in. It was 3 o'clock when we finally made it. I tidied the sails while Adrian and Andrea went to check out the restaurant and café.

They came back with bad news. The seafood restaurant was closed for a private party and the café had stopped selling hot food at 3 o'clock. Eating on board did not appeal, especially with the squally wind and Kippa bouncing, so Adrian and Andrea sensibly decided they would get a minicab back to Truro.

Meanwhile, I took refuge in Mylor church as the heavens opened again. I had a short nap on a thoughtfully placed pew cushion and then played the piano which had the full set of notes. It was out of tune but each octave made sense on its own so I attempted to follow a compact theme to exploit the pretty F sharp. There was nobody about to spoil my illusion.

When the rain stopped I decided to try and get to the Pandora Inn. With a mix of gentle engine and a slice of jib, Kippa and I were there in no time but as we neared the wooden quayside the rain started to streak down fiercely. Just metres away from the jetty Kippa grounded. I did not panic, knowing we were on a rising tide. I waited for a while and then a passer-by kindly took a rope and tied me on. He left me to sort out the details and I pulled from the bow and gradually Kippa slid across the mud. I warped the stern and set some spring ropes and then rushed into the Pandora Inn as the rain tumbled down. The effort to get to the pub had been worth it. With an affable smile from the bar and an imaginative menu on the board, it was a paradise on this awful night. The décor was tastefully traditional, the tables clean and the chairs comfortable. I indulged in a belly pork and scallop starter, then a seafood linguine and finally a brandysnap basket with ice cream and sorbet. Terrific. A coffee might have rounded it all off but none was offered so instead I struck up conversation with a retired couple from Mylor who had a Cornish Crabber, a modern yacht in a traditional style. We talked of St Just and drying out our boats on the seashore and were soon at our ease. We discussed the dangers of lightning and I learned that earthing a boat increases the risk of a strike but that with no earth there is the potential to explode if you are hit. I did not get much rest that stormy night.

Sunday morning started with more heavy rain after a brief interlude of clear sky. I put away Rolly, the new name Adrian had suggested for the dinghy, and set off with a strong following wind. With only jib up, Kippa flew along at 4.5 knots. Past King Harry's Ferry I raised the main and had a wonderful sail right up to Truro, only bringing down the sails as we entered the final stretch. The rain had stopped and even Tesco's could not spoil the view of the cathedral.

While I was relaxing by the quay an elderly couple came along and showed interest in Kippa. They came aboard for a cup of tea and it turned out that they were Margaret and Frank Dye, who are famous for their extensive sea travels in a Wayfarer and whose boat, Wanderer, an open dinghy, is featured prominently in Falmouth Maritime Museum. They talked interestingly about their exploits but, equally, were keen to find out about my plans. They warned me against Portreath in North Cornwall where a large swell that had not been forecast nearly wrecked them on rocks. Margaret was dead against North Cornwall but Frank mentioned the allure of the harbours with a glint in the eye. I found them very unassuming, modest and warm-hearted people and when they left I felt that Kippa and I had been given their blessing.

I returned home at the beginning of October to close down my recruitment consultancy but found worse news. The transport research firm was losing some key government contracts and we faced an abyss. I had planned to appoint a managing director to run the business in my absence but now it was obvious that it was not viable in the long run. This was not what I had planned. If I took time off to cruise in Kippa next summer then I would be coming back to no job and no income. I reassessed everything, considered restarting the recruitment business and thought about whether I could sell the transport research company as a going concern.

When I returned to the boat on Friday 13th October the tide was neap and there was fog. In gloomy mood and poor conditions we set off down-river and picked up a mooring in Malpas Reach until visibility improved. The weather pattern was now high pressure but with a low trough expected to spoil the weekend. I watched the fishermen and then set full sail. It was a good passage right down to the Carrick Roads, and I took a business call by mobile phone while full sail was up. Kippa and I came up under the lee of the St Just-in-Roseland peninsula and I took down the main for a steady and comfortable sail up the Penryn River just on the jib.

Keith and Jim, two friends from the Abbey Sailing Club on the River Thames, came aboard for the weekend and we did some fast sailing, reaching six knots near Falmouth, before finishing off with a good meal at the marina. They helped me pack up sails and on the Monday I took Kippa up to Ponsharden Boatyard to be lifted out for winter.

Time at that boatyard had a surreal affect. I did not feel I belonged amongst the regular sailors. I was not really a yacht sailor at all. I was a dinghy sailor who had a yacht temporarily. I had a big trip in the planning and yet I had so little experience. They knew all about anti-fouling and winterising and so on. I knew nothing. I was not afraid to be a nuisance though and people were patient in explaining the basics. During the autumn I got help with servicing the engine, took the sails to be laundered and had to face a rotten time at work.

Back at my place of work in Wimbledon, my staff were fantastic during a difficult phase of the business. Brian Street, who had worked for the firm for many years as a survey supervisor, stood out most of all. He shouldered the burden of the worst part of selling the company. He spoke to all our field workers and gave them the news. It was an heroic task and one that he did simply because he felt it was the right thing to do. The work he did was enormously respected by everyone.

10. Penryn to Penzance

Spoiling it for Super

To get my equipment from Surrey to Cornwall, my local car dealer, Bell and Colvill, kindly leant me a Sloane tractor which was fantastic, swallowing all Kippa's gear in one go and still performing like a race-horse. After getting Kippa prepared, I went home again to finish off business matters.

At the time I was suffering the grief of losing my business and therefore livelihood. I had been a business owner for 20 years, a transport researcher and employment consultant. With little yacht skippering experience I was very much a landlubber who had pottered in the Solent, I was now 48 years old and embarking on a journey which was probably beyond my capabilities. I had taken sailing courses but these can never replace experience of time at sea.

So it was that by train I returned to Ponsharden Boatyard on 7th March, 2007, taut with apprehension, a rare coldness inside. I did not feel cut out for the trip ahead. I was an office worker, not a sailor. Fortunately, Michel, the boatyard manager, was hospitable, although he still doubted I would get much beyond the harbour entrance. It was a reasonable view. I doubted it too.

I settled into Kippa once she had been lifted out into the water and made the best of a wet and windy night. At least the morning was bright and boded a day of pleasant weather so I cast off, tested the engine and then pulled alongside a sailing school yacht and spoke to Nigel, one of the instructors. We had a quick chat about twin keeled boats and their windward performance. His amusing comment was that gentlemen do not sail to windward.

I got the sails rigged with the help of the sail loft and then welcomed two people from the RNLI (Lifeboats). They carried out a free inspection of equipment called "Sea Check", provided some sensible advice and seemed to tick all the important boxes ˒n the safety list. After a chicken, mushroom and rice supper, Keith arrived so we had a drink at the bar before settling into our berths on board. I spent the night troubled by the prospect of the next day. The forecast was reasonably favourable though when we got up in the morning squally showers were blowing in from the north.

Keith is a retired police superintendent who is utterly reliable. He had agreed to come down to Falmouth to help me get started so I was keen to get sailing and achieve an important first leg of the season with his help. I still had tons to learn about having crew on board and the day turned out to be learning by bitter experience.

A blue sky replaced the clouds and it was time to be off. We raced along in the lee of the Lizard Peninsula, but what would the Point itself be like? I felt I could not let Keith down by bottling out now, even though I would have gladly anchored in a bay and returned home. If we had, perhaps I would never have turned that corner. We did turn the corner, but there were casualties.

As we came out into open sea the waves built up. It was rough but not too confused. I passed the helm to Keith because I was concerned he would get seasick. It was a fatal mistake. I was seasick instead.

We were heading west and downhill. Keith was now in charge while I suffered more and more. We ploughed into Mount's Bay where it became choppy rather than rough, but I could not recover. I just moaned and felt like death. As each wave hit I groaned miserably and began to shiver. I entered a microsleep as we came down each wave and was then jolted awake as we hit the crest of the next. It was torture for me but for Keith I think it was much worse. The only thing worse than torture is watching somebody else go through torture. Later, Keith told me that it was only fear that kept him from being seasick. At the time he was typically courageous. He battled on for hours and hours, using the engine to speed us in as fast as possible. Eventually I was so exhausted that I did sleep as the sea calmed. St. Michael's Mount appeared but receded as darkness fell. Now Keith was faced with Penzance, a harbour he knew nothing about, and he was approaching it at night.

There were no buoys to lead us in. Which were the lights of Penzance harbour? Keith discussed his concerns while remaining calm. I took the helm for a short time and then managed to pull myself together sufficiently to go below and check the chart and almanac. We closed in on the fixed green and red lights of the port. Keith did the hard work of getting fenders and warps on and without any complaint. Much relieved, we entered the Wet Dock. Keith was finished, but remained in control of how he felt which must have been pretty bad. He deserved to be angry, ill and shattered but he did not show it. I was recovering. I wonder if poor Keith ever will.

We ate some old fish that I doubt was Cornish and, on Keith's advice, I drank cola which I have to admit is a good pick-me-up in such circumstances. The sugar rush and the clean bubbles, I suppose. We slept well that night.

11. Penzance to St Ives

Armed Knight

My Achilles' heel is my constitution. I like to think my strength is my planning.

Sir John Harvey-Jones used to relate a story, which I recall being about two identical factories to be built, one in Britain and the other in Japan. The aim was to be up and running in two years and after six months the British claimed good progress. The site was cleared and the building had started. By that stage, the Japanese had done nothing on the ground and were still discussing, talking and planning. Eighteen months later the factories came on stream at the same time but, while the Japanese production ran perfectly from the start, the British struggled with teething problems.

It is fun to plan as you go along with the thrill of multi-tasking but if you want to maximise your chances of success at sea it is better to plan, review and plan some more, especially if you are like me and make silly fundamental errors. I have often muddled up hours, days and even months when taking information from the tide tables in the almanac; however, if I do the calculation three times and then three more times using different base data, I am in with a chance of getting it right.

In the case of the inventory, I wrote a list, then I wrote a separate list and compared. Finally I went through the list with my daughter, Rebecca, and placed each item within the boat on a diagram, simultaneously marking up the inventory. That way, not much got left behind when we set sail for the first time.

Now in Penzance, I wondered if all the planning and preparation had been a bit pointless. It had been such a dreadful trip from Falmouth I seriously questioned the sense of going further. Thinking of everything I had given up and how much I had committed to the project just made me feel low and rather stupid.

Even when rested in the morning I was ready to pack it all in. I talked to Keith and asked him what he really thought. Was I really cut out for sea sailing? He gave a very sensible and measured response, suggesting I did not make an immediate decision but nevertheless should keep the dream alive while reminding me that even getting to Penzance was an achievement in itself.

What really clinched it for me was when Keith suggested that I take things stage by stage and set myself smaller targets. Perhaps I should set the realistic target of getting to Milford Haven, which would be much further than most yachtsman from the South Coast venture. It began to make sense. I could not get my head around the vast size of Britain but Milford Haven might just be possible.

We took the bus up to Marazion to enjoy the views of St Michael's Mount. We walked over the causeway at low water and studied the quays along the harbour edge which helped to lift the spirit as we planned where to tie up Kippa for a soft landing on the sand.

As it turned out, I never reached St. Michaels Mount by sea, even though Kippa was so close and it had been on my list of top ten places to go if ever I were to sail round Britain. It is a magical spot but not one I have conquered.

I could not find words to express my enormous gratitude to Keith but deep down I think he knew how I felt when we said goodbye. I had let him down terribly, not for the first time, because this was now the third trip on which I had been seasick with him on board. Truly a friend in need, he has said since that I owe him nothing. In fact, I owe him a great deal.

What I did not realise was that though the trough I was climbing out of might be deep, the lowest point on my travels in Kippa was still to come.

On the Monday I tested the outboard motor. It had seized up so I took it into a marine engineer to see what he could do while I went exploring Penzance. The High Street has chain stores you could find in any British town but if you climb to the top and then fork right you discover the "Green Market" with a mix of new and old independent shops, including a hardware store and a super organic greengrocer and grocer. Retail therapy worked and when I returned to the boat the outboard was fixed. I sought out the artistic side of the town and found the art club and an organic restaurant but they were closed. I ate on board and felt open to the idea of continuing.

As morale lifted I made up my mind to take advantage of neap tides and a more settled forecast. I checked the tides again and confirmed the time to make a start in the early morning. Putting the Lizard behind me, I went to sleep more relaxed. I awoke in the middle of the night and was now itching to move on. I got up at 2 am and prepared myself for Land's End. Just another headland, someone had said. Would that be true or would it prove worse than the Lizard? I was on my own now to find out.

The wind was force two to four and from the north west. The sea state forecast was for slight to moderate. Kippa and I left harbour at 4 am with a small trawler for company in the early minutes of the voyage. I piloted by the navigation lights and admired the twinkling stars. At 5 am a soft and silky half-moon rose as we made our way round the coast. When the moon slipped under a low cloud bank I sensed daytime looming. We reached the Runnel Stone, which we gave a wide berth to avoid the tidal race I had been warned about. We were motor sailing in a light wind, but would the wind be stronger as we came alongside the rocky dangers of Longships? The tide was running with us at one knot when the sun brought some warmth, outlining the shapes of the fair weather cumulus clouds. Dare I take the inner passage, inside the dangers but where the sea may be confused? Kippa felt magnetically drawn to pass Land's End. The spectacle of spray on the rocks of Armed Knight, a double jagged set of rocks that were sharp enough to pierce the most hardened vessel in the world, was entrancing. The sea below was beginning to bubble and churn as we approached the cauldron edge of Kettle's Bottom. I could imagine the guests in the hotel looking out and seeing this lone yacht and reaching for the bell to call the waiter. I could imagine the young waiter reassuring the guest that all was well and there was no need to call the coastguard. At least not yet.

It was a thrilling experience, more so after the disasters of Lizard Point. We were skating along the lips of such devilry, the monster snoring, spitting, hissing gently in his slumber, unaware that prey was passing overhead.

With relief and pleasure we sailed out to sea to give the Brisons and Pendeen Point a wide berth. We were on schedule for tide and I was taking no risks now. The sea was calm until a moment when quite suddenly the Atlantic showed its face. We were truly out in the ocean now with nothing, except the Scilly Isles, between us and America. The wind had picked up and I was sailing confidently though a ground swell began to sweep under us. We were turning the corner now, heading east north east and I was grateful that the wind and tide were not in conflict as the long wavelength swell gently shook Kippa as if the Land's End giant was lifting his morning robe.

I began to feel very tired so I put on the motor and the autopilot to take a break. I searched all around and could see no activity. I checked we were out of any shipping lane and had a very short nap and a few minutes' reading.

We gradually came closer to the coast and I began to seek St Ives. When I found it, the peninsula did not seem to jut out as far as I expected. The western beach seemed quite small. We came round into the bay and went alongside the massive sea wall. It was a pretty spot but Kippa did not like it. She surged back and forth, even though the swell did not seem strong. Long lines fore and aft could not dampen the effect and the harbourmaster said that springs would do nothing to help. By the time I had understood how unpleasant the surge was, it was too late to pick up a mooring buoy, although I later discovered that the surge even there meant that as you dry out you get beached with a series of nasty bumps.

It was no good, I decided, I must seek out a bed and breakfast if I was to sleep that night. It was a long walk up the hill in search of somewhere with a vacancy at a reasonable price.

Up and down the lanes I went until I was running out of ideas and came upon the rear entrance to a guesthouse. I dropped down through the garden to find the back door. I was let in by the landlady and shown to a comfortable room.

Once I had relaxed and settled in I became hungry and set off again down the hill to the town. On Adrian's recommendation I tried the Seafood Café. Expensive and uncomfortable, clean and stylish, it was certainly somewhere different. You choose your fish and then you choose your sauce. The result was a large portion of healthy eating that almost succeeded brilliantly.

12. St Ives to Clovelly
Dolphins and cliffs

Tom Wood, another friend from Abbey Sailing Club, is one of those rare people who are virtually fearless but also blessed with common sense. Formerly a nuclear engineer, he is a practical and down to earth Glaswegian, who came down to St Ives to sail with me up to Swansea. We had a week or so to do it in.

In the Bristol Channel tides run fast and tall, funnelling up the Severn Estuary. To progress from one port to the next with six hours of tide in our favour we had to start at low tide. Most harbours in the region can be accessed only around high tide so our timing would be important.

After I met Tom at the pretty little station tucked under the cliffs, we had to release from the quay and anchor in St Ives Bay, where we would remain afloat in deep water and be able to pick up the morning flood tide that runs north east.

We set off at 7.15 am with a slight to moderate sea and a force three to four wind. It was dry with some cloud but breaks of sunshine too. Soon after we had turned out of the bay and were making our way up the coast we came upon a magnificent pod of dolphins. Within minutes there were groups of three, four and five dolphins all around us, around 50 in all. They were making their way like single-minded commuters on the 7.48 from Croydon to Waterloo but a couple did take time to come up to look at us briefly, one turning its head and directly eyeballing me. They had a quick swim in our bow wave before rejoining the procession. The grace and intelligence of these mammals are very obvious up close and reminds us humans of our inadequacies.

We continued on past Newquay, surfers' paradise, enjoying the sweep of Cornish coastline, to the River Camel. At the entrance there were many rocks and islets to avoid before crossing the "Doom Bar", which is notorious in a strong onshore wind. By careful pilotage we avoided trouble and entered the port of Padstow, taking up a berth close to the town but then moving to the outer wall on local advice that there would be better depth of water there. The gates to hold in the water after half tide were being repaired so we made ready to take the ground and dry out on sand.

Padstow is a pretty place but is so overwhelmed by the Rick Stein effect that it has lost its original identity. Making the best of it, we sampled the Stein fish and chips and, it has to be admitted, they were superb. Crispy, tasty batter and very fresh fish.

To progress north the next day we once again had to work our way out at low tide. With a distance of 44 miles to travel to Clovelly, we set off at 6.15 am and initially pushed against a foul tide. The sea began slight and the wind light so we used the motor for the first hour to keep up to schedule. Then the wind grew to force four, then five and we were flying along past Tintagel and Boscastle as the sea changed to moderate and the notorious swell built up. Hartland Point was the crucial tidal gate, sticking out like a knuckle north of the famous surfing beaches that face west from Bude and beyond. Overfalls were marked and we had a choice of an inner or outer passage. We saw a few more dolphins and fishing boats but then a coaster came shooting up inside us and made short work of the headland waters. We took a careful inshore course and got ourselves under the lee of land as soon as we could. Wind had now reached force six and we were down to jib alone, firing along at full speed of five knots, riding the waves, working hard to dominate the environment to arrive at high water in Clovelly.

The harbour is completely invisible even from quite close to. Yes, there are settlements, which are obvious to locals, but for visitors there is very little to go on.

One clue, however, was a Dutch ship which was anchored at a spot recommended by the chart so we took our bearings for a settlement that appeared to be where Clovelly should be. We closed into the coast and then closed up to the cliff but there was still no sign of a harbour. Then at last we could pick out a sea wall with houses behind. We were less than half a mile away when we finally identified a cliff and then a lifeboat house. We had a particular cottage to aim for and had been told to be accurate in our steering, leaving the tall sea wall to starboard by a boat's length but no more. We came in and turned 90 degrees as explained by the harbourmaster whom we had called in advance. When we came alongside the quay there were enormous wooden piles and ladders that suggested we had entered another century. The harbour-master was there to catch a rope and guide us to a precise spot. He congratulated us on our accurate entrance and we settled in. As the tide went out, we realised just how critical the entrance was, there was hardly any room for error at all. By the sea wall there was a pile of dangerous rocks , then a gap perhaps only 15 metres wide, then more rocks.

We had a shower in the excellent lifeboat station where the harbourmaster also worked, before taking a well earned pint in the inn. It was pleasing to discover that Kippa was the first yacht of the season to enter Clovelly just as she had been at St. Ives.

Clovelly is a tourist trap but out of season and out of hours you can enjoy the village. The High Street climbs the cliff past pretty old cottages, village shop, another inn, studios and front gardens with well tended flowers. Where the hill turns at the top of the High Street is an adorable pink house with a very pleasing symmetry that is not ostentatious enough to be grand but is too elegant to be merely pretty.

13. Clovelly to Bideford

Get out while you can

Tom, Kippa and I had enjoyed some reasonably fair weather to bring us up the Cornish coast. However, the pattern was on the change; gales from a northerly direction were forecast. Clovelly is not the place to be when this happens. Strong winds of force six were predicted for Saturday and force eight for Sunday. The harbourmaster politely suggested we get out fast, if possible.

We began to make preparations and brought Kippa down to the end of the quay to be in the deepest water possible so that we could get away before high water. We had decided to head for Bideford, the only place of refuge on this coast for many a mile, but the challenge was to get across the notorious Bideford Bar before the tide turned. If we were late and the river began to ebb, then we would hit breakers and be unable to get in.

We set off from the wooden pier and as soon as we were out of the shelter of the sea wall we knew we had our work cut out. Tom was at his best, enjoying the challenge of raising the sails in the tumbling sea. In seconds, Kippa picked up speed.

About halfway across the bay, the swell grew and grew as the wind increased. I clung to the tiller which was pulling hard on the crests as the wind caught the sails with full force and then went slack as we fell into the troughs. We had the mainsail twice reefed but kept some jib out to maintain maximum speed but it became impossible to control when a particularly strong gust caused Kippa to lean over beyond her gunwales. She broached uncontrollably into the wind as the rudder lost grip and the hull shape took control. I slipped off the seat and onto the floor. Kippa slid down the wave with most of the starboard side of the boat in contact with the water but almost none of the port side. As the wave passed and we found ourselves on top of the crest, I regained grip as the wind hit us harder still and we heeled right over again. We crashed into the next wave and the sea came over the coach roof and landed on top of us. I fought to find an acute angle that would carry us up and down the waves while Tom chatted away under the spray hood as if out for a Sunday afternoon stroll. I found his calm demeanour very reassuring and this meant I could concentrate on the task.

All the time I was aware that if we did not make good progress we would be unable to get into Bideford. There was no port of refuge short of Milford Haven, at least 60 miles away and against the wind, which equated to at least 20 hours' hard sailing, including through the night across a busy seaway! We pressed on as hard as Kippa could manage, cutting across the swell as best we could.

We picked up the estuary buoys with the binoculars and found the entrance to be well marked. We turned so that the wind was following and began surfing like crazy, still two reefs on the main and now just a handkerchief jib. Either side of us we could see the breakers rolling across the beaches, particularly so on a sandbank on the starboard side of the channel. We crossed the bar just before high water and had enough push to help us up to Instow, where the channel is less clear.

We followed the Appledore quayside and found it all rather unpromising so continued up the River Torridge. Eventually we could see a bridge that meant we could go no further. The quayside of Bideford was a real mix of craft, from sailing boats to tugs to fishing boats and other commercial craft. Unsure where to moor, we looked around and chose to come alongside a big steel yacht called Lucia. By luck, it turned out to be a sound choice, we dried out onto hard mud without tipping over too much as Kippa's keels sank in.

We were glad not to have been caught in Clovelly because the wind continued to increase through Sunday until the hurricane in the Atlantic sent its tail through and hit the whole area with a hell of a storm. Despite the shelter of the town, the quay and other vessels, Kippa pulled hard on her warps, rattled her mast and tossed us around all night, making me feel distinctly queasy. Even Tom did not sleep as soundly as usual.

Looking back at the log I wrote on the first day or two in Bideford, I see that I found the shops rather characterless and downmarket. However, the place grows on you. There was an exhibition in the museum which offered little until I stumbled upon a photography section. Ski Harrison deserves to be more widely acclaimed: she has the ability to capture people in a remarkable way. Her work began in Devon where she created portraits of old people in all sorts of settings, from helping a cow to give birth to preparing to sweep a chimney. The character of the subjects shines through strongly while recording how people can be active even in the later stages of life.

Ski Harrison went to India and Africa and recorded a series of scenes that epitomise communities, demonstrating her ability to engage with the local people and put them at their ease in order that they relax and be themselves in front of the lens. Her later work focuses on children, in Britain and abroad, picking up on their play and naughtiness in an amusing and engaging way.

Venturing further, I saw a three-masted wooden ship and then, beyond the bridge, Tom and I walked along the old train track, now a cycle and footpath, which follows the curve of the river that itself becomes more interesting where man has not interrupted the variety of rush and meandering flows which have created salt marshes and rapids.

By bus, I went to Barnstaple and enjoyed its special flavour of North Devon. A town with the confidence to consider itself a local capital, it has a vast market building, many interesting shops and a style that is all its own.

Tom and I ended up in Bideford most of a week – first because of the weather and then because the radio stopped working. We had a look to see what might be wrong but could not identify the problem. Fortunately the harbourmaster knew someone called John Rice who turned out to be a highly skilled and extremely helpful marine electrician. John was aboard Kippa within hours of our call for help. He tried the radio and then opened up the electrical panel. He didn't like what he saw but was too much of a professional to say anything. I was rapidly gaining confidence in him and so I asked his advice. He felt a rewire would do no harm. He explained his thinking and then next morning fitted a bar for negative returns, tidying up as he went along. What was impressive was how he worked with the circumstances presented to him. He did not rip things out, he coaxed and cajoled wires, adapting and improving, working out the logic of previous work, accepting what was good, tackling what was not. He left to continue a project at Ilfracombe but returned in the evening to progress with a colleague in tow. About to return home, he smelt a problem on the deck, by instinct he unscrewed an aerial connection and found things loose which should have been soldered and secured.

The next morning he came back and fitted new fuses and lent Kippa a radio while the Standard Horizon set was tested. John engendered complete trust, partly through his skill and partly through his personality, which was natural and unassuming. Never willing to accept second best on any aspect of the job, he fixed everything electrical. Better still, he explained each stage and encouraged me to follow his work so that I could tackle problems that arose in the future. Even now, months later, I have a wiring diagram of Kippa in my head and when I needed to change a cable for the chartplotter that had perished, I was able to sort it out with just a quick piece of advice over the phone from John.

14. Bideford to Swansea

Sandcastle memories

Early on Friday morning Tom, Kippa and I set off, sailing against the incoming tide in order to arrive at the Bideford Bar before the ebb began. The wind was brisk and we made good speed but once into open water we found ourselves heading into the wind and therefore having to tack up the coast. The tide beyond the bar was with us initially but within about three hours it had turned against us. I had hoped to reach Woolacombe to anchor but it became clear that Croyde was our best option. We found a spot with reasonable shelter where we could get some rest. We took turns to watch that we were not dragging anchor and I prepared a baked potato, cheese and beans to provide a filling meal.

By the time we were ready to leave at 2 pm the wind had died and we were forced to use the motor. We passed Woolacombe and Putsborough which brought back memories of my grandmother who helped me build a sandcastle there. I was only about four years old but I can still picture the steps leading round to the top of the keep of that magnificent fortress.

We saw Ilfracombe in the distance as we headed across the Bristol Channel. It was a pleasant crossing, passing two ships at anchor, but by the time we were within sight of The Mumbles the red sunset strip had faded and it was night-time.

I checked the almanac and noticed a comment about barrage opening times. I called up and they confirmed that they closed down at 7 pm. The best they could offer was a waiting mooring. This experience taught me to be more thorough in reading the almanac when planning. In Bideford we had been pondering how to get up to a harbour of the North Devon coast before crossing to Swansea but, with a northerly wind and time running out for Tom, we had ultimately decided to make a big step instead. There was still no excuse because I could have checked the almanac earlier in the day.

Along the Gower Peninsula the wind increased and we were sailing well, kept alert by adrenalin as Kippa picked up speed. A night entrance to Swansea is not straightforward because the bay is full of lights for 180 degrees. Picking out navigation signals from street and house illumination is almost impossible and the most hopeful sign we could identify was some vertical blue lights. These were not marked on the chart but were on the bearing where we expected the port.

Making full use of the chartplotter, we managed to find a navigation buoy as we headed up what we believed to be the channel. It became obvious the blue lights had to be the port despite looking more like cinema advertising.

Once past the piers we negotiated the harbour amongst yet more ambiguous lights to discover the two buoys used for waiting boats. We tied on and settled in after a long day; we were too tired to worry about not being able to get ashore.

15. Swansea to Tenby
Beach night

First thing the next day, Tom and I got Kippa in through the barrage lock and on through the marina lock. I dashed up to Sainsbury's to stock up and then booked a taxi. The taxi driver was late and the excuse given was that his firm did not recognise Swansea Marina office as a location. When eventually I got into the taxi that had been driving up and down outside the gates, I was told off for not telling them I was at "The Boat-yard". I explained I was a visitor without local knowledge. The reply was that I could walk if I preferred. Nice welcome to Swansea.

I met Sarah at the station and we took a taxi back with a more pleasant driver who gave us the inside information on how the young people of Swansea spend their evenings. Conclusion? Move on.

Sarah came on board and we said goodbye to Tom, who waved us off from the lock. The sun was out and the sea was calm. A gentle breeze was wafting in from the east and we had a pleasant sail around The Mumbles. The wind fell away and then switched round to a stronger westerly, which had not been forecast. We sailed on with the aim of Burry Port, Sarah helping to helm, gaining confidence as Kippa leaned, her forefoot streaming through the water, dancing up and down over the waves. I watched the GPS and saw that the tide was soon to turn. Our speed through the water was increasing but pleasure was turn-ing to struggle. Time to take in some sail and, not a moment too soon, I was pulling on the reefing line as Sarah tried to control the tiller. We managed somehow then tacked back towards the coast. I recalculated the trip and decided the best plan was to come into Port Eynon Bay and anchor. We found shelter and calm water close to the beach.

Sarah was doing well but not feeling her best. I baked potatoes and grilled some steak which we washed down with a little red wine. Sarah refused pudding so then I knew she was definitely below par. Afterwards I had a little nap in order to be alert for the night sailing.

We set off with stars and moon in the sky and very few lights on the coast. I called up the coastguard to give them a passage plan to which they responded by asking if I was sure that Burry Port was open. I said I believed it was but if they knew something different I would like to know. They then went off and checked, came back and said that it was open but that the lifeboat station had reported that a night entry for someone new to the estuary was not wise because a crucial navigation light was missing.

I had gone to a lot of trouble preparing for Burry Port, collecting information about the shifting banks and the ideal time to enter the harbour, but now I needed to rethink the situation. The coastguard suggested I consider anchoring and going into Burry Port in daylight, however, when Sarah and I talked it over, we decided we preferred to try and get to Tenby. With the westerly wind I knew we would never make it there by sail alone and it would require the motor to make sufficient speed on a close hauled motor tack to have any hope of getting into the harbour while it still had water. Tenby had always been the place Sarah wanted us to reach and it was a harbour I had long wished to visit from the sea.

We told the coastguard our plans and they asked us to call Milford Haven coastguard on our arrival. We pushed on and the sea became choppy as we entered the more exposed area of Carmarthen Bay. I persuaded Sarah to take a break, go below and lie down. She had not rested up to now and I was concerned she would become unwell. She soon settled into a solid nap while I pushed Kippa along against the waves.

Carmarthen Bay is like Mount's Bay; it has that never-ending feeling. The lights on the shore are hard to identify and the far side does not become clear until you are almost across. Halfway there, Sarah came back on deck and was keen to take part again, feeling more chirpy. I gave her the task of spotting navigation buoys and before too long we were on course for the first flashing light. Encouraged by this, we felt Tenby was within our grasp. I recalculated the timing and saw that it would be 50/50 as to whether we would get into the harbour. However, we need not panic as we could beach or anchor; with the westerly wind that was blowing we should be protected in the lee of the town.

That first flashing navigation buoy light haunted us for hours. We battled on towards it for ages before a second light that was charted not much further west appeared. Almost immediately afterwards a third light was visible and now we had to distinguish the three. From a distance this was not simple and staying on the bearing kept us busy. There are rocks and islands protecting Tenby so the pilotage is tricky; it is easy to make a mistake and be wrecked here. It was past midnight before we reached the first light, which meant that it was now unlikely there would be sufficient depth in the harbour. We continued on and threaded our way up to Tenby amongst the rocks and islands. We were not home and dry yet though; a symbol on the chartplotter had appeared and we could not be sure what it was. We felt we had to avoid it. We got closer and closer but could not make out anything in the dark. I kept saying that there was something but Sarah kept saying she couldn't see anything. Time pressure was tremendous. We might still have a little water left to get into the harbour but also there was a danger of rocks below the surface further along the beach if we headed away from the charted obstruction. We kept looking and worrying until finally I said: "Well whatever it is, we are going over it now." We were held in limbo, expecting a bang just as a ship expects to be hit by a torpedo, when we saw a boathouse and realised the structure was right below us in the water. We looked down at the water between us and the shore and could see a ramp disappear into the sea – it was the slipway for the lifeboat and we were only just going to clear it. We continued on, then turned in close to the end of the sea wall. There was just a pool of water left by the end of the sea wall but most of the harbour was dry. We were within spitting distance of the quay and I thought we might just make it when we grounded before we could even throw a line to pull ourselves in. The wall by the first ladder looked rough and so I threw out the kedge anchor as best I could to be able to pull ourselves away from the harbour wall when the sea level rose again. There was no way we would get any further on this tide.

I put the alarm clock on for early morning and we settled down for the night as the last of the tide ran out. Three hours later I got up and assessed our position. The harbour was now completely dry and the lines of mooring chains glistened eerily in the pale light. I got out of the boat, climbing down the stern to reset the anchor where it could gain purchase, though realising that with the many chains laid in the harbour we might have some problems. At about 6 am we were both up and enjoying the strand of sleeping town with its graceful pastel coloured buildings, rising three, four, even five storeys. The beach curved around and then stretched out towards Saundersfoot and we could see the tide rushing towards us. The wind had turned back to an easterly and was blowing briskly, pushing in waves under our keel. At the first possible sign of movement I pulled on the anchor chain to swing us round. Kippa was lifted up on the swell just breaking onto our sides, floating us for a moment before dropping us back down. Sarah and I then had a very uncomfortable 20 minutes being lifted and dumped unceremoniously back down onto the beach. It was an awkward predicament with the anchor doing little to help us. I put the engine on and tried to find a way to get out of the spot succeeding only in dragging and then snagging the anchor. Meanwhile, the quay still did not have enough water. Fed up with the shuddering and worried it could start to harm the keel bolts, I managed to ease Kippa out to deeper water to where she would stay afloat while letting off anchor chain. Suddenly it dawned on me that I could release the anchor quite safely and pick it up at the next low tide. I undid the rope from the chain while poor Sarah did her best to keep us out of trouble but was struggling to keep Kippa away from danger. When I let the anchor go I found myself at ease, even though it seemed a bit drastic; I took the tiller from Sarah and motored us out into deeper water where we could wait until there was sufficient water to get alongside the harbour wall. As soon as possible we came back in and got ready to climb the second, more robust ladder; at this point someone who must have been involved with the harbour in some way – we were never to find out – came along and took our bow rope. More skilfully than anyone I have seen before or since, he put the warp around a bollard, pulled in the bow, put the warp around a bollard further back and then threw me the rope, telling me to take it and pull it in. I did as I was told and Kippa drew into the quay perfectly. He had rigged a balancing effect that caused the yacht to line up parallel quite naturally. The man was gone before we could thank him properly.

We stepped ashore and sought a café for breakfast. We found an ideal place but it was not yet open so we had a wander. It was a great feeling to have made it to Tenby; we knew we had achieved something worthwhile together and the town brought back happy memories for us.

The café overlooked the headland which jutted out, parting the beach and leading the eye to a glimpse of Caldey Island. I had hoped to land at Caldey but I also feared the island's harbour which could quickly become untenable.

We explored Tenby and then had to make our way down to the railway station. I accompanied Sarah on the little local train that chugs through the Pembrokeshire countryside to Carmarthen. We said our goodbyes and she went on to Burry Port to change for Didcot while I returned to Tenby, now on my own for the first time since St Ives. It was a strange ride back, empty and lonely, as the train trundled through the little valleys, past washing lines, small trees, fields, gardens and streams, the view – mostly man-made but occasionally natural where allotment gave way to marshland.

As soon as I got back to Tenby I wanted to find the anchor. I also wanted to keep myself busy straightaway so as not to dwell on how sad I felt. People looked on, wondering what I was up to, as I dragged the chain this way and that, length by length, amongst the mooring lines laid in the harbour. I cleaned off the sand and mud and got the tackle stowed, then had a final exploration of the many facets of Tenby, a town where you can always get lost and then find yourself again but facing a direction you did not expect. When Patrick McGoohan, The Prisoner, escapes from Portmeirion it is in Tenby where he will be washed up and wonder if he has discovered civilisation. I hope the Birmingham accents will reassure him.

16. Tenby to Llanion Pill
Return to the Rectory

There were still remnants of a south easterly when Kippa and I set out from Tenby. As you head west, there is a shallow channel between the mainland and Caldey Island which can be negotiated safely with care and settled conditions.

A friend of a friend who lives on Caldey was due to give me a wave but I never saw her, though I waved at the island harbour in the hope that she could see me. Caldey was very enticing and if there had been time in hand I would have attempted landfall. However, I wanted to use the good weather window to make progress because the next stretch of water had many hazards.

Apart from the usual issues of tidal races and unsettled seas, there is a busy firing range along southern Pembrokeshire and I had been advised to keep well out from the coast if live firing was taking place. Kippa sailed for the first couple of hours but the wind died to nothing at all and the sea became smooth so we had to motor. We passed a larger vessel, a small commercial ship, and from that I knew we were far enough off the Castlemartin range to be safe. It was a quiet lonely voyage from there until the entrance to Milford Haven, where one or two tankers were moving. What wind there was at this stage was easterly so I chose the anchorage of West Angle Bay, which is tucked in the eastern side of the entrance to the Haven. A peaceful spot, there is enough rise of land largely to blot out the industry, leaving only a couple of signs of habitation.

I chose my anchoring position with care, wanting to rest peacefully for the night. I made sure the large anchor took hold and paid out sufficient chain to cope with a change in the weather. A strong westerly might have meant I needed to move but there were no signs of that. Once settled, I watched the birds, admired the colour of the rocks and studied the appearance of a sandy beach within the rocks where a stream flowed out. If I had had the dinghy deployed, I would have ventured on land. Instead, I waited for a fine sunset and then made a meal on board.

The 13th April brought more fine weather: a pleasant easterly was breathing down the Haven and this encouraged me to tack Kippa against the wind up the Cleddau Estuary. It was good fun to cross this important shipping channel exploring the shallows at the sides, seeing the depth plunge in the middle, choosing when to tack to miss rocks off a fort, deciding when to play safe and when to take a calculated risk. Jetties being built to receive liquefied natural gas tankers were the principal obstructions and we got close without having a scare. Gradually the wind strength became more fluky as we progressed; the hills were blocking the wind which was trying to funnel between them. The width of the sailing area was decreasing and the tide was soon going to turn against us. I was keen to keep sailing as long as possible in these sheltered waters that were a pleasure to be in, but eventually time and tide were against us and we had to motor the last stretch under the tall road bridge at Pembroke before turning to starboard and into Llanion Pill, just a touch after high water.

Kippa was lifted out by the boatyard just after midday. I had calculated that the extra cost of being taken out of the water was largely compensated for by the saving in mooring fees. I wanted to look at the antifouling and the propeller anyway and sure enough, the antifouling had peeled some more, though the prop was fine.

The boatyard owner was very pleasant and did his job competently enough so I would be able to relax while in Andalusia seeing Monica and Becky.

That last evening before the Easter break I spent with John and Fiona Cutting. John picked me up and after a long bath at the Old Rectory we went out to a pub for a meal and very enjoyable chinwag. Despite the disruption of floods that had spoilt their flooring, they made me very welcome and I slept soundly in the comfortable bed. The sparkling river views in the morning were at their best as I tucked into a very substantial breakfast of sausages, bacon, eggs, tomato, crusty granary toast and flavoursome real coffee. John dropped me at Haverfordwest to catch the train home.

17. Cadiz to Solva

St. David's Cathedral

A week's holiday with my daughters in the warm sunny South of Spain had been arranged so that I could take a break from cold British weather. Not everything goes to plan. While we had a week of cloud and cool conditions in Spain, Britain continued to have fine sunny weather. Nevertheless, it was great to be with the kids and the temperature was pleasant for most sightseeing, if not ideal for the beach.

The highlights were Granada and Seville. The clouds broke up sufficiently for us to appreciate the gorgeous blue light that bathes the Generalife gardens in a way that makes them lift towards Heaven. In Seville we were impressed by so much of the architecture; I particularly admired the stained glass of the cathedral.

Returning home to England, I was picked up by Sarah from Gatwick Airport and next day we went down to Poole to see Joanna, her daughter, perform with the National Children's Orchestra in an almost professional way, a couple of pieces by Walton being especially bewitching.

Two nights in idyllic weather at Sarah's house meant it was tough to get back on the train to Wales. However, after another night with the Cuttings and a chance to discuss the merits of Jack Sound I was ready to be on my way again. Launched again, Kippa and I made our way to Milford Marina for the night in order to be positioned for tide to take us north along the coast. Milford has a convenient retail development right next to the marina and this was a chance to ensure that the galley was up to date.

My next aim was Solva, a tiny village, but I had hopes of a stop at Skomer Island to watch the seals. A kind man at the chandlery at Milford gave me advice and an old chart of Jack Sound and then after a buzz round the supermarket I spoke to John and Jan in a Moody 31 for further local information. On top of what John Cutting had explained, I was confident of the next step.

Kippa sailed out briskly and all went well until mist gathered. We got through Jack Sound with reasonable visibility but I did not fancy being anchored at Skomer in a fog patch so we continued across St Brides Bay, taking care to avoid any tankers that might be inshore.

The entrance to Solva is one of the scariest in Britain, protected by large jagged rocks. The main pinnacles do not seem to cover at any state of tide so the danger is obvious; the sea swell can carry you from one to the other in a single swoop. We powered in with sail and motor, relieved to make it to the calmer water inside. After a bay with a beach, the entrance turns 90 degrees, giving excellent shelter. The visitors' moorings are not obvious and when I picked up a small buoy I was immediately hailed by locals. It was not an unfriendly shout and they kindly explained the local situation. We were on a private mooring but would be allowed to move to another mooring which belonged to the caller. He communicated that each position consisted of four "legs", something I had not seen before. There was a rope loop for each corner of the boat so that you were held perfectly in position. It took a bit of fiddling but was as snug as a full harness seatbelt once connected.

I had expected Kippa to dry out quite quickly but it took ages before she touched bottom. I was suffering a bit of cabin fever having been on dry land for Easter, so at the earliest moment in the morning I climbed down the transom and waded out from Kippa.

I put my trousers on, climbed the little hill towards the main road and stuck my thumb out at the first vehicle I saw, a Land Rover. It stopped and the driver took me to St David's while he chatted about his family and kayaking. A very different character from me, much more rugged and practical, adventurer rather than office boy on a jaunt but we found common ground when we talked of New Zealand.

Arriving at the cathedral, clothed in a thin gauze of pale morning mist, was joyous. Tranquil as a remote parish church though full of birdlife with the dawn chorus at its finale, the setting of St David's is the chief delight. The church lies in a hollow by a babbling brook with a hilly churchyard bordered by some fine mature trees on one side. Opposite there are lovely old cottages, the ruined abbey and a piece of land that is neither garden nor farmland, appearing entirely natural, a delicate balance of nature where flora and fauna coexist happily.

The building is of subtle dimensions formed of Celtic shapes which create a very Welsh harmony. The soft, pastel coloured stone gives off a warm glow that draws in both mind and body. Everything inside and around has been treated with gentleness and good sense; the windows are elegant, the proportions human, the décor unfussy, the gardens tended but not overdone, quite a contrast to the intricacy of the Mezquita of Cordoba or the awesome pomp of Seville's Cathedral. It feels as if an evolution has taken place where each generation has respected the past – even the new organ takes its place comfortably.

Beyond a small museum filled with gracious goblets, you walk through lovingly restored cloisters to discover a café with a mezzanine floor which seems to float on air to gain best vantage of the building's exterior features and its surroundings. It is a miniature masterpiece in its own right where you can sit and enjoy fresh wholesome food such as nutty crusts of which the monks would have been proud.

Returning to Solva by bus, I noticed a fishy smell that was sweet and more appealing than the usual harbour odours. With the tide still out, I walked up the hill on the south side of the harbour from where I could see a crescent beach and the entrance as well as the curve of the scoured channel. It was a useful way of checking the route to take on exit.

Tenby, Pembrokeshire, Wales (*above*), Llangwm, near Haverfordwest (*below*)

Fishguard, Wales (*above*), Kippa perched on boulders in Cardigan (*below*)

Aberdovey Estuary, Wales (*above*), Strangford, Northern Ireland (*below*)

Isle of Eigg with Rum in the background (*above*),
Port Mor, Isle of Muck (*below*)

Isle of Eigg, one of the Small Isles in the Hebrides

Findhorn, Moray Firth (*above*), Portsoy Traditional Boat Festival (*below*)

18. Solva to Fishguard

Surfing the reefs

It was an afternoon start to catch the best of the tide through another significant tidal gate. The sea squirts between Ramsey Island and the mainland and if you try to go through at the wrong time you get pushed backwards.

Kippa and I curved round the edge of the harbour along the channel which I recalled seeing at low tide, then slid out through the rocks and along the coastline. We passed beaches below St. David's where Druids, Vikings, Celts, perhaps even Spanish might have landed in the past to shelter from a north wind that might have carried their longships or galleons down from the Irish Sea. When we reached Ramsey Sound I could see a line of little breakers. I was glad not to be coming through with a sea swell. I followed the plotted course, looking for a break in the line of white water, but there was none so I picked a spot that seemed the least turbulent and went for it. Sometimes the sea was swirling round, creating completely smooth water on top, then you could see it rushing north, then it might be bubbling or breaking. It was fascinating. The GPS told me that the stream rate was four knots but as Kippa came through the worst of the white water it must have increased to seven knots because the log spinning on the hull was showing a speed of only three knots through the water while the GPS said ten knots over the ground. There were rocks strewn around the island and close to the coast so I had to maintain an accurate course, though it was difficult with such pretty views of the island.

As Kippa sped north, popped like a cork from a champagne bottle, we passed a black and white fish with a fin that might have belonged to a porpoise. It was a pleasantly swift sail before we reached Strumble Head with its distinctive lighthouse. We turned into the bay, left the main port of Fishguard to starboard and searched for the old harbour.

The entrance is not well marked, but there are not too many dan   ⌐ if you are sensible, and Kippa was soon able to turn in under the main quay and find strong wide ladders with rings on poles that we could tie to so that we could rise and fall with the tide without surging backwards and forwards as we did at St Ives, for example. Kippa dried out on a bit of a tilt, but we were on our own and nicely settled. Everything was well set up including a convenient hose on a reel as well as shore power had I needed it. Even the yacht club bar was only 30 yards away, which would have been ideal for Tom, with a selection of beers: smooth, very smooth or really smooth. Chemically adjusted gassed alcohol did not attract me, nor even a sherry that might not have been touched since the Coronation (Queen Victoria's). The locals were not particularly friendly, which is not a criticism of the Welsh because there were English voices among the group. There were a couple of young lads on the pool table who were happy for me to join in and have a laugh, so that is how I passed an hour.

In the morning I was able to take a shower in the clubhouse before considering my options. There was fog and it was quite thick so I went in search of a Sunday lunch venue or a shop. There was nothing, just a drinking pub, so I went for a walk up the little river.

The first thing I found was a very Welsh sight: a babbling brook amongst the trees and a very ordinary cottage alongside with a garden full of rubbish, the detritus of 30 years of family life and forgotten adventure. There was a little fishing boat that was never going to sea again, an old bicycle, a swing, toys and various other bits and pieces that "might come in useful one day". Although it was a mess, you sensed the family who lived there were a happy bunch.

I continued along the well trodden path, ignoring a staircase of soft green that perhaps the goblins had created, for it seemed to lead nowhere except into the hillside. I discovered a profusion of wild garlic spreading from the water up the banks of the dell. Through the trees I spotted the houses become tidier and fancier until I could see a grand mansion that would have been perfect if it had not been spoilt by a conservatory extended to the side. I picked some leaves and flowers of the wild garlic which was ever more luxuriant in the marshy bog, and then returned to the boat to make my lunch.

I was settling into a routine aboard, the weather forecast being the dominant theme. Via a plastic covered aerial on the stern rail, the Navtex receiver produced a listing of the shipping forecast on a screen at the chart table. Programming the device correctly was far from intuitive but at least I was getting a general idea of the weather from it. However, for a more detailed picture of the local weather, I listened to the coastguard who broadcast an inshore waters forecast. Generally I found the morning forecasts were accurate for the day. Predictions the night before were more likely to be right than wrong but a forecast of weather more than 24 hours ahead was not reliable.

I looked at longer range predictions of weather patterns via the internet and used the BBC site, the Met. Office, the "Magic Seaweed" site, which gives a nice view of swell (wave height), and the German forecasts via Frank Singleton's website. These were useful in predicting the gales at Clovelly but, in many other cases, they were of no help at all and, after a day or two, the weather charts for three or four days ahead would change significantly. This made being up-to-date very important and as time went on I came to listen to every bulletin the coastguard provided during the day and sometimes at night, if I was awake.

Entertainment was the radio or reading. The hi-fi, a car radio, worked well but received FM/AM only so I invested in a portable Sony radio so that I could listen to Test Match Special on Long Wave. I found the portable radio so good that it almost took over from the hi-fi. Using it did not deplete Kippa's domestic battery and I could place it wherever I might be on the boat. In the evening I could curl up cosily in the aft cabin with Scruff, a soft toy dog that Sarah had given me, and listen to "The Archers" though I would usually sit or lie on a saloon bunk to read to take advantage of a good halogen reading light.

I kept Kippa spick and span throughout the voyage. Cleaning lifted morale even in the darker periods that were to follow. Cooking an appetising meal was something to look forward to and the excellent little cooker did me proud. In the oven I could roast or braise; the grill was adequate so long as I kept an eye on it and the two burners of the hob gave out lots of heat or, instead, could simmer away for hours without drying out a pan.

19. Fishguard to Cardigan
False start

The tide had turned and the fog was lifting on a gentle breeze. I headed out of Fishguard with electronics turned off to practise my navigation. However, soon after we had left the harbour under sail, the wind died and mist enveloped Kippa. I motored along, picking out the headlands one by one, studying how groups of birds behaved as the mist thickened to fog.

I put the electronics on and checked my position, then pushed on to reach Cardigan on a rising tide. There was an eerie peace, as calm as the Serpentine in Hyde Park, until a porpoise suddenly appeared.

To enter the Cardigan estuary you follow a bearing towards a large hotel, then hug the shoreline beside a caravan park and then nip round a sand spit. The channel turns in and there is a floating pontoon, designed for dinghies I imagine, but with nobody about in the early evening gloom, I tied Kippa on.

I liked the spot, a sort of treasure island with beach on the exposed side of the spit, despite the fact that when you walk further along you come upon land where mobile homes nestle in the dunes, the people inside watching Coronation Street, oblivious to the hairy, smelly being from a yacht peering in.

I looked back at Kippa to see if anyone had seen me, rather as one might watch to see if a traffic warden was noting down your registration. There was nobody so I had a stealthy look in at the yacht club. There were one or two people packing up to go home. I did not bother them because I wanted to remain incognito.

On the morning tide we made our way up-river, following the tortuous route of the marked channel. As Kippa progressed, the scenery improved. St Dogmaels is a delightful village, spread out across the hillside, the unplanned mix of houses and bungalows, a ruined abbey, working buildings of farms, all creating a harmonious tapestry of shapes, sizes and colours. Again I noticed the lack of a dull uniformity that blights parts of many English villages and instead was sensing the Welsh spirit redolent of Dylan Thomas. The Ferry Inn turned me away from their wooden quay but advised me I could moor on the public pontoon marked "No mooring", so I did. I could blame the locals if anyone bothered me, but they didn't. I decided to walk from this point into Cardigan. I was now in amongst the houses and bungalows, chapel and sheds of various uses, looking across the river at the humpy fields and mixed woodland on the opposite bank. I made a half-hearted search for a bus stop but soon walked on to see what I might find round the corner. The waterside had boats here and there, including a large wooden gaffer, while the village streamed on until its ribbon just touched the outskirts of Cardigan.

It is a forgotten county town with a diluted status but its pride is still intact, the past is cherished and modernism has not been allowed to overwhelm. The isolation from Cardiff and London means Cardigan struggles, needful of aid here and there, while exuding a character shaped by people wanting to be off the beaten track. Cardigan is at the end of a rail line that was ripped up years ago, the track now converted into a cyclepath and footpath to link up with a nature reserve of marsh and coppice wood. A new small theatre that houses a super café creates a centre to the town and the shops are individual and interesting. The castle was on the mend.

At the end of the day Kippa and I slipped back down to the floating pontoon but this time I knew I was going to meet authority because three men in yellow jackets were hovering. They were helpful and although they did not really want me on the pontoon, they let me stay without charge on the basis that I was leaving in the morning and kept away from any fishing boats landing.

The next day the spring tide was in full flood and Kippa's warps were struggling to hold on as the water ripped through. By almanac calculations I needed to leave but by observation now was not the time unless I wanted to risk a messy accident. I watched carefully until the speed of the tide lessened a little and I sensed there might be just sufficient depth of water.

When I let go the ropes I only just managed to turn Kippa. Before we could go any further the keel touched bottom. It was momentary and Kippa was lifted off and could continue. However, the tide was flowing very fast past the spit and we could not make headway mid-channel. We pushed across to the far side where I judged there was sufficient depth in hope that the water might be moving less quickly. Sure enough, we edged ahead until we were able to get beyond the point. A few yards on we dashed back across the channel to hug the coastline where the channel continued. Confidently I raised the sail and passed Cardigan Island where I found the wind was right on the nose and the open water was cut up. I calculated that in these conditions I would be doing little more than two knots along the rhumb line, the direct course to my next stop. Even with favourable tide under me, Aberaeron was impossible, even if I used the motor to help.

I decided it was the moment to turn and run. I swung Kippa round and began surfing back, swirling around on the awkward wavelets caused by wind being against tide. I doubt the wind strength was more than force four but I was feeling distinctly queasy and was relieved to get back into shelter. I made my way up the channel again, past St Dogmaels this time to take advantage of the height of the spring tide to reach the little quay in the centre of Cardigan Town. I was happy to step off in familiar surroundings, my only concern being the state of the river-bed when the tide ebbed.

I watched and waited, noticing that there were boulders on the bottom. I looked to see which would be the best spot to choose, ready to draw Kippa along the pontoon if necessary. I did not like the look of it. Anything I could see was not suitable, each rock being big enough to catch one keel but none big enough to support both keels. Finally Kippa began to take the ground, sliding away from the pontoon a little. Then she stopped and the river washed away and she was left perched precariously on both keels, each on its own boulder.

I visited the town again and did some more exploring, reading my e-mails in the old library before making a meal and then having a peaceful night like an elf sitting on a pin. I was comfortable and settled in Cardigan and it was going to be difficult to rouse myself in the morning.

20. Cardigan to New Quay

Prop knot

On 18th April the spring tide flowed with rubbish. Not as strong as the previous year at Saltash when the tide had brought down 70s memorabilia, this tide was still high enough to dislodge branches and other vegetation as well as some man-made bits and bobs. In amongst it was also seaweed that had been brought up from beaches.

Kippa began struggling out against the strong flow and it was while I was trying to avoid catching the propeller that there was a thud that sounded like a log hitting the hull. I put the engine in neutral and then back into gear. There was no apparent problem so we continued and got ourselves out to Cardigan Island. The wind had virtually disappeared and the sun was out. We were motorsailing, enjoying the coast which was looking its best beside the blue and benign sea. I kept the motor ticking over but we were not making good speed through the water. I was worried – had something got caught around the shaft? Or was it engine trouble? I monitored the smoke and water coming out of the exhaust. Was there more smoke than usual? At anything above four knots the engine was straining and causing the water to turn dark, which was a bad sign. I throttled back and we chugged along gently looking for wind, but there was nothing worthwhile. I recalculated. The time taken to get out from Cardigan Town plus the slow progress meant that Aberaeron was again not possible. Aberystwyth was a long way further on and even that was not an all-tide port. I considered the options. Pwllheli was the only fully accessible harbour but that was right across Cardigan Bay, at least 12 hours away, probably more. I called up Aberaeron harbourmaster on the mobile phone and he confirmed I would be just too late to make an entrance safely.

I had picked out Aberaeron as a beauty spot and discounted New Quay because it was hardly a harbour at all. There is a breakwater and then a bay, unsuited to any kind of west or north wind. Even nor'-east looked bad. However, there was still no sign of significant wind. What about depth? It was a very tidal harbour and calculations showed that it was a marginal option. I pressed on carefully and kept recalculating, making full use of the chartplotter to judge speed and distance.

When I discovered New Quay, the first thing I saw was the fish factory, not an inspiring sight. Nevertheless, I was keen to get in if I could, in case the engine failed. We turned the corner at the end of the pier, eased in gently, watching the depth which was getting very shallow, only to be confronted by a new problem. The sea wall I intended to tie against had ropes trailing from it and some boats moored to those ropes. The rest of the sheltered area of the bay was full of small vessels including some yachts. The good news was that most were floating and we still had a few minutes to make a decision. I searched around for options and was wiggling amongst the moorings when two locals cheerfully waved for me to go through a gap where there was just one mooring available. I picked it up and they came alongside in their dinghy to help. Only half an hour later, Kippa was beached. We had been lucky.

When I explained my concerns about the engine to the friendly members of the yacht club, they put me on to a marine engineer in a pick up truck who I feared might be more muscle than skill. He said he would have a look later when the beach was dry and so I took myself off to find a crab sandwich and an ice cream. It turned out I was completely wrong. The gentle giant, assistant coxswain of the lifeboat, was very happy to help. He had a good look and put his weight against the shaft but found nothing amiss. He did notice that the rope cutter was shiny and suggested that something may have got wrapped around the propeller but had eventually been cut off. I think he was right, because when I next used the motor everything was back to normal.

The afternoon weather was idyllic; the sun was not just shining, it was hot and was baking the west-facing beach. I had a swim in the sea and then took an invigorating run right round the bay. Looking back from the far corner, I surveyed the scene. The village had offered little but the location was very pleasing in this kindly weather.

During my trip it was often the case that clouds had silver linings and I began to take the philosophy, encouraged because I was reading The Alchemist by Paulo Coelho at the time, that if something went wrong it might lead me somewhere that would be worthwhile. Here was a case in point. New Quay is not recommended in the almanac, but in settled weather, or in an easterly, it is a lovely spot.

21. New Quay to Aberdovey
Breaking the rules

The engine started well in the morning, which was a relief because there was, again, little wind. My plan was to continue to Aberystwyth, the most important port along this coast, where I could visit a chandlery and get to know the town better.

Kippa and I passed Aberaeron, close enough to get a good look with the binoculars. Then I telephoned the marina at Aberystwyth to check that they had a chandlery that sold charts. It took some time to get through and when I did I was astonished to find there was no chandlery and nowhere to buy charts. Now I was stuck. I had not expected this setback. The best advice I could get was that Dovey Marine in Aberdovey might have something. I was surprised that such a minor port might have charts but anyway I needed to make a snap decision because by now we were well past Aberaeron. We could go into Aberystwyth but then a day would be lost making a short hop. With fine weather I was keen to press on, so I quickly recalculated to find that we could just make it in time to reach the quay at Aberdovey. I rang their harbourmaster and took local advice that confirmed it would just be possible in the time although it would be a very tight schedule.

I adjusted our course to cross the shallows, one of several banks in Cardigan Bay that extend like roots under the sea from the mountains overlooking this stretch of coast. I reckoned that we should arrive at 11.50 am and then allowed 40 minutes to travel the final 1,800 metres to the jetty, expecting a strong ebb in the estuary. Tidal predictions turned out to be accurate and we passed over the estuary bar as predicted. However, as Kippa entered the gaping mouth, the ebb was even stronger than I had expected. I glanced at the magnificent mountain backdrop and the pretty Georgian houses but not for more than a moment because I had my work cut out if we were to reach the town's quay. Though Kippa was doing over four knots through the water, the tide was knocking nearly all that off and she was hardly moving in comparison to the houses. Another decision to be made: should I abort, with just 1,000 metres to go and head for Pwllheli, or should I press on somehow? I decided to take a gamble, a crazy one in hindsight, thinking I could apply dinghy experience in rivers to this tidal estuary. I drew Kippa out of the channel and headed for shallow water. If Kippa grounded the tide would rush out and Kippa would be high and dry, wrecked even. However, I hoped that the flow was so fast and our progress so slow that if Kippa touched I could stop engine and the flow would carry her back off. I watched the way the water behaved to see if I could assess where there would be sufficient depth. It was madness but it began to work as our speed over ground climbed from 0.7 knots to one knot, then 1.4, then 1.8 knots. We passed a starboard hand buoy on the wrong side and not by a yard or two, but by at least 30 metres. I wondered if local people might be noticing that I was cheating, seriously. We continued on, the aim being to keep up a speed of no more than 1.5 knots so that we would not hit a sandbank hard and might still have flow to carry us off, balancing the demand to make sufficient progress to get to the quayside before the water depth had dropped too low. We passed another starboard hand buoy by an even wider margin, perhaps 40 metres, and then I decided it was time to cash in our gains and make a dash for the opposite bank. I was worried by the look of the water up ahead; it was like a washing machine and I did not fancy a soaking, so I immediately turned Kippa towards the channel. Of course her speed over ground dropped. By the middle of the channel Kippa was going back downstream but I knew we were also getting across to the side of the channel where we would ultimately need to be. I hoped that the jetties I could see ahead might be blocking the tide. We crawled to the edge of the beach. Here it was even more dangerous to go out of channel because I sensed the stones, which I could almost touch, shelved steeply, so we hugged the edge of the marked channel, only easing fractionally out of it when essential. We were making headway and sure enough we reached the jetties.

When we got there the layout was not what I had imagined from the plan in the almanac. The jetties were tall wooden structures and I could see no way of tying to them safely. The quayside was rusting metal, hardly more attractive than the doubtful piles, and while assessing all of this we were having to dodge moorings and boats tied on to the moorings. Trying to control Kippa in the swirling, rushing tide was proving increasingly difficult.

Just then, a man called from up above. I had to assume he was the harbourmaster. He gestured for me to come alongside the rusting metal. I found a few metres of clear space and then started to get fenders on. It was not simple because when I came out of the cockpit I had to leave the engine in neutral so, naturally, Kippa would slide back. I had a race to get each fender on and back into the cockpit before we got caught up in a mooring. I did not run along the deck but I wasted no time as I tied fenders one by one.

The bow warp was harder still because it meant going right to the front of the boat, tying the rope on and getting right back along the length of the boat before Kippa was out of control. I took Kippa right up to a mooring to leave space aft to fall back into and then pushed the engine control lever to neutral. I walked briskly up the side deck while Kippa kept going forward towards the mooring. Should I go back to the cockpit or would she fall back? She did neither, she turned but just enough to miss the mooring before she began to fall back. I put the warp on and looked round. Now Kippa was heading broadside towards a fishing boat on a mooring. I could sense people on the quay watching. I may not have heard their gasp as Kippa closed in on the fishing boat but I saw that one person was about to shout as I got to the cockpit and jumped on the engine's gear lever to shoot Kippa forward. I was not yet holding the tiller and so although I put power on, it was undirected. It was only a second or two before I had got my hand on the tiller but it was long enough for power and tide to create a spin. Worse still, I was disorientated as we headed towards more danger. I sensed the audience gasp again as I let Kippa fly downstream towards the jetty, away from the fishing boat but towards ruin. I pushed the tiller away and Kippa span again, this time to be parallel to the quay. I eased up alongside a ladder amongst the rotten quay, ferry-gliding in, bit by bit. The harbourmaster was ready to catch anything I threw. I put Kippa in neutral again, judging the moment when Kippa might stay head into the stream for a moment. She did and I was able to throw the line.

Aberdovey has a big tidal range, not quite of the scale of the Isle of Man or Bristol, but big enough. Half tide had long passed and now it was a long way up from Kippa to the harbour master standing on the top of the wall, arms outstretched. My throw had to be good. I might not get a second chance. I looped the line and left some on the deck and threw. It just reached and the harbourmaster grabbed the line, fumbled but held on, then managed to get the line around something. Kippa's beam was right by the ladder and I took advantage of the situation by climbing up with the stern rope to tie on aft. Kippa and I had survived and we had arrived in Aberdovey. I swore never to take such a risk again but I was glad I had. The scenery was stupendous.

22. Aberdovey to Pwllheli

Prisoners of the weather

After a dangerous landfall, I needed a walk. Further along the estuary past a gentle cove with its single wooden dinghy I discovered a delightful path that threaded over rocks and amongst the gardens of Victorian mansions. By chance I came upon an inn called the Penhelig Arms. I noticed some rather posh people going in which suggested it was somewhere special; when I looked at the menu it seemed fairly priced so I went in. Despite my bedraggled look I was served handsomely and fed the best three-course meal I can remember. The service was absolutely spot-on, timed to perfection so you never felt hurried or forgotten.

20th April brought more balmy weather. At first the wind howled down through the valley and Kippa was able to sail out of the estuary to the open water of Cardigan Bay but as soon as we were a mile away from the river-mouth the wind died. I had planned to take a route west and then north but the sea was so calm that I decided to make the most of it by following the coast so that I could see Harlech. The treacherous off-lying reefs extend many miles but there is a gap just by the seashore. I took this way and we came close up to the beach. Beyond I could just make out Harlech Castle, a stronghold of the English that had once looked down from the cliffs to water below but was now well inland where sand had been deposited and a lagoon created. I was tempted to go into the lagoon and anchor for the night but I decided to turn Kippa west and continue to Pwllheli. One day I would like to return to the region and explore this coast right up into the corner where Porthmadog lies.

It was a long crossing but an easy one with the sun bringing enough heat for me to peel off sailing jacket and trousers. Entrance to Pwllheli was not difficult but I was glad of advice from a man in a dinghy to avoid a silty stretch.

The marina was large and impersonal and felt out of place in this distant corner of Wales. It turned out that many of the locals did not really want it there because it brought English people to the area. It was a shame. Had the opportunity been fully embraced then the port could have been an enormous success. It would have taken great skill, though, to create something that was harmonious with the location, not simply a commercial venture. Exceptional architecture would have been required to make it attractive. The yacht club did have some welcoming faces, fortunately, and here I met Gordon and Sue, who have since become friends.

On the 22nd April the weather changed for the worse. The beautiful early spring was over and the dreadful summer of 2007 had begun. From this point the trip started to go badly.

On the Sunday another friend from Abbey Sailing Club arrived, having travelled by train from Oxford through the Welsh mountains and along the coastal line from Machynlleth. Morris Weightman is a very good-natured and easy person to have on board, making no demands and fitting in very easily. He did not let the weather worry him, even though he had come many miles to go sailing. When the weather turned very foul and windy we took the train to the sheltered nook of Portmeirion which was looking splendid with its spring flowers. The following day the weather was no better so we headed off again to see the Talyllyn Railway. It was a long trip along the coastal mainline railway but the scenery was spectacular. We were too late to take the little steam train up into the mountains so instead we walked. Amidst the wet and windy day there were breaks in the rain and we had a bracing walk. We waved to the steam train as if we were the Railway Children, then huddled under trees for lunch before exploring the fields and farms. The Talyllyn has not attempted the ultimate realism of some historic railways, even though it was the first to be preserved. Instead it has chosen to be the prettiest, most dreamy and romantic. From a daffodil glade by a tiny station we followed a footpath along the river, discovering a farm on a hillock with views to sea and mountain. A more idyllic spot could not be imagined, the house poised in cosy isolation on a grassy bank above the rushing river.

23. Pwllheli to Port St Mary

Morris majors

After three days stuck in harbour, we set off on the Thursday with Morris having only two full sailing days left. We would have a task on our hands if we were to get to the Isle of Man.

Much planning had gone into timing the next two tidal gates, Bardsey Sound and Caernarfon Bar. Gordon, Sue and other club members gave me lots of local advice; the island of Bardsey has a rocky, shelving edge and round the southwest corner runs a very significant tidal race and, to avoid it, there is a passage between the island and the Lleyn Peninsula. Within this passage is a rock called Carreg Ddu.

We arrived at the first critical point precisely as planned, sailing with full rig. As we turned from southwest to north we began to head into wind but with tide carrying us forward I felt confident that we could tack through the sound safely. As we came closer, I saw that the space between Carreg Ddu and the land was tiny while the strait between Carreg Ddu and Bardsey Island was wide enough for a ship. I decided we would go through the narrow gap, tacking. I was on the helm and Morris watched, commenting that he had never been so close to treacherous rocks. I had, at Solva for example, and reckoned that these rocks presented no problem in reasonably calm seas.

During the morning the wind had been steady but as we continued north, the wind dropped and our speed fell. With a notorious tidal gate ahead, Caernarfon Bar, we put the engine on to keep the speed up. The scenery was fine and the weather fair but by late afternoon it was beginning to get tiring cutting through the uncomfortable short waves.

As we approached Caernarfon Bar we sought the navigation buoys. We knew that the chartplotter could not be relied on because the sandbanks move so regularly, nor could our paper charts help us; we had to identify the first buoy by eye. Working hard, we managed to make out one, two and then three buoys. What we could not positively identify was a fairway marker to show us the entrance. We chose to go for the most westerly buoy and round it closely, watching the depth. It worked out but it was a hairy half-hour until we could be certain we were in the channel. It is at times like this that one realises why there are so many wrecks around our islands. Judgement can take you so far but there is an element of guesswork and therefore luck when coming into an unknown port.

As the day closed we reached Caernarfon. There was the castle, the town and the marina. At this point I decided we should press on for Port Dinorwic. It was the wrong move.

The tide turned at Caernarfon and pushing against it became a struggle as time ran on. It was very late when finally we reached the lock gates and got ourselves into the sheltered basin. Having pushed the engine hard to get this far I wanted to check it and, on inspection, I found the belt to be a bit loose. At this moment we should have gone to bed but instead I fiddled around without really improving matters. Poor Morris had no time to settle down, though he did his best by taking a short walk and having a beer before turning in. We missed out on supper, beyond feeling like anything to eat. Another mistake.

If we were to continue onwards the next day we had only one daytime option to get through The Swellies, tidal whirlpools and eddies where the water churns along the Menai Strait cascading amongst rocks and shooting rapids between the bridges. If you get your timing wrong and arrive late you go backwards and the water can easily throw you onto hazards. If you are too early, the tide is so fast that you lose control. The window to get through on Friday 27th April was 7 am to 7.30 am. That meant rising at 6.15 am to have time to get through the lock gates and up the Strait during slack water.

We managed it and Morris looked happy on the helm as we passed under Britannia Bridge at 7.30 am. He was pleased to be sailing at this point. After I had piloted us through The Swellies and the Menai Bridge I took over the helm as we continued north east. The wind was dead against us, funnelling down between Anglesey and the mainland, making it awkward to tack in the narrow channel. At this stage I made my third bad decision. I should have realised how tired we were and chosen to take us into Conwy or Beaumaris. However, I was tempted to continue by a good forecast for a north easterly wind which would give us a nice reach right across the Irish Sea to Port St Mary.

I took Kippa up to Puffin Island at the end of the Menai Strait and headed out into the Irish Sea where she made excellent speed. I tried to optimise the angle to the sea to make it fast but not too bumpy. I realised I was getting very tired and not feeling great so I passed the helm to Morris and went below to lie down and get a few minutes' rest. I usually find that even just ten minutes' rest enables me to recuperate; however, as I got below I felt rough. I lay down quickly but it was too late. I was very sick and felt awful. I tried lying down again but it did not help much and my pain just worsened from that point on. They say that seasickness is equivalent to poisoning and it certainly felt like that. Poor Morris was on his own on the helm now. He managed well at first but as minutes turned to hours and I did not improve, he began to be concerned – for me, for our safety and for his own ability to cope. He is tough but he was as tired as I was.

I kept trying to get into a recovery mode but found myself in agony. The movement of the boat was really hurting now. Morris did his best for me and in fact did very well at keeping me from sinking deeper. Eventually though Morris was getting to his limit. We managed to get the autopilot out from its box and I groaned instructions on its use. He got it fitted and all was well for a while until he accidentally pressed the tack button. The autopilot turned the boat through the wind with Morris not realising what was happening and, imagining the boat was out of control, he was nearly knocked over as the boom came across. I should have told him to be careful not to touch that button and although Morris did tell me off, he stayed calm when he had every right to be angry.

The situation stabilised and now Morris was able to cope better. He still had to remain alert for shipping but at least he did not have to hold the tiller. Unfortunately the autopilot and chartplotter began to drain the battery so he had to put the engine on to ensure that we did not lose electrical power.

The next problem that Morris faced was navigation. The chartplotter showed our direction to be west of our aim. If we continued as we were then we would hit an island called The Calf of Man, instead of reaching Port St Mary. I tried to reassure Morris that the east-going tide would get stronger and sweep us back to Port St Mary but he did not seem convinced. He took my word for it but of course he could not be sure I was *compos mentis*.

We ploughed on with the Isle of Man in sight but still a long way off. As another hour or two passed Morris started to struggle again and needed me to take a turn at keeping a lookout. I was still feeling dreadful and found myself unable to get up. My head was achi   s if being hit by a lump hammer. My body was shaking and every part of me wanted to give up. I just could not find the willpower to get on deck. I felt like death. Morris asked how much longer it would take and I gave him an honest guess, three hours more. He asked again about our direction. Our direction had moved slightly east but we were still not heading for the port directly. I was still certain our course was right but I let Morris move the setting slightly east to keep him happy. Morris battled on bravely until he reached a low where he asked if we should make a Pan Pan call, which is a lower level call than a distress, but serious nevertheless. This finally got me to realise how much of a liability I had become. I just had to pull out of it so I got up and struggled into the cockpit. I told Morris to take a rest but he was not prepared to do so. He could see I was a wreck and he did not trust me to keep a lookout so we agreed on a compromise. He would stay on deck but shut his eyes while I sat at the top of the companionway where the movement is most bearable and where I could get a good view. I looked around in all directions and Morris sensed I was able to manage, though he wisely told me to disturb him if I had any concerns.

I doubt that I gave Morris more than a half an hour of break – it may even have been less – but it was something. He recovered a little and perhaps I did too. The island finally started to grow in size and our course was now bang on Port St Mary. I adjusted the course back west a little so that the cross-tide would take us in precisely. Morris was relieved to see that my navigation had been correct. The sea began to settle down, although it had never been rough throughout. I was becoming human again and was able to read the almanac and the charts. Between us, we struggled into harbour and alongside a high seawall. The range of tidal height is enormous in the Irish Sea but we managed to get up the ladder and tie up to the bollards.

I had let Morris down very badly but he was brilliant about it. He put on a very brave face and made no criticism even though I had made some really dire decisions. He had been left completely in the lurch but he had ensured our survival. I felt particularly low because Morris was the second casualty I had inflicted.

You would think that I had learned my lesson. In one respect I had. I was never going to subject a crew to that situation again. This I have achieved. However, at that stage, I had still not discovered how to sail Kippa and not be seasick myself. If crossing to the Isle of Man was bad, crossing from the Isle to Northern Ireland was even worse – in fact so bad that I decided to pack it all in when I reached Portaferry in Strangford Lough.

24. Port St Mary to Portaferry
Accepting defeat

On the Saturday Morris took a taxi to the airport to return home while I caught the old steam train to Douglas. I was still feeling very dicky and the wobbling train did not help even though the scenery was pleasant. It was good to see the island's capital again; it is an interesting place, being traditional but not tacky. The money that has flowed in with the financial services business has kept the place in generally good order.

I did some shopping, including a visit to Marks & Spencer, which had just been refurbished with high-tech lighting that transformed the mundane packet of biscuits into a treat. I visited the chandlery at the harbour for sea bands, another attempt to combat seasickness, and then tried the station café, which had excellent, wholesome and home-made fare.

Kippa was surging back and forth in the harbour when I returned and, still feeling delicate, I did not fancy a night aboard so I walked along the beach to a bed and breakfast.

Much refreshed by a good night's sleep, I decided I had to try and conquer the seasickness. The weather was fair with a force four to five still blowing from the northeast. The harbourmaster and I talked through the options of Port Erin in the next bay and Peel Harbour on the west coast of the island in case I could not cope. He was very helpful and supportive, checking with his counterpart at Peel about the tidal situation for later in the day.

When I set off I felt he had given me all the boost he could and wished me well in a genuine way. He was a sensitive and kind man who realised I was struggling with my adventure.

Once beyond the pier I raised sail and headed south-west around the

Calf of Man. The sea was certainly moderate but I was coping reasonably well and was pleased I had had the energy to try again.

I chose a course to take me into the lee of the island where I might get shelter from the wind if it became stronger, but this proved to be unwise. At times the wind did drop but then it would funnel through the hills and hit me. The sea changed from a long wave pattern of moderate height to a meringue shape with heaps of water with no particular form. Worse still, an occasional large wave would appear from an unexpected direction and toss Kippa over. There was no way to predict what might happen next and the confusion was doing my head in. I tried a run and a broad reach to the wind. On a run I could manage but on a broad reach it was unbearable. The problem was that my direction to Strangford Lough demanded a broad reach. The next error I made was crucial. I put the autopilot on to try and get a break. The result was that my brain could no longer make any sense of the boat's movement and I was seasick. At the time I did not realise what I had done, I just felt miserable.

Without a crew I just had to make the best of it. There was shipping about and I had to remain alert. I wasn't though. I had a good look round and then went below and lay down for about two minutes. I judged I dare not be below a second longer and was soon up again, looking round. I felt worse and worse, more and more exhausted, my head pounding incessantly and my stomach retching with nothing left to vomit.

About an hour from Northern Ireland I decided enough was enough and made a final resolution that I was going to stop this madness and put an end to my suffering. I focused on how I would sell Kippa and told myself I only had to get into Strangford Lough and I could relax because my voyage was nearly at an end.

Some horrible hours later that I hesitate to recall, Kippa reached the entrance neck which leads up to Strangford Lough and we were carried in on the young flood tide, racing up the channel, past wheeling water, to Portaferry and a set of pontoons that call themselves a marina. The man in charge was brisk and informal and we were soon settled.

I called Sarah and told her that I was fed up and wanted to pack it all in. She did not try to persuade me to carry on but instead just praised me for having got as far as Northern Ireland. This was the best thing she could have said. It took the pressure off and helped me focus on what I had achieved rather than how I had failed.

The yacht club, in a little terraced house, was open and I received a sociable welcome. John McAlea, the commodore, sorted me out and put me in touch with the ferryman who could provide a free mooring.

25. Northern Ireland

The day I went to Bangor

The image I had of Northern Ireland was conflict. Film of armoured cars, people throwing stones, buildings on fire and provocative marching seemed to bring pointless loss of life. Through the smoke and flames one could see bravery, cowardice, hopes raised and dashed.

I arrived trying to be neutral and with eyes open but was shocked to see Portaferry. There was a general sense of sadness caused by the occasional burnt-out house or derelict shop. In what must be a backwater, I thought things might not be so bad. In Belfast or Armagh I would have expected it but not in this little village.

But as I spoke to people, my mood was lifted. They were courteous and helpful as I asked the way to the launderette. It was, in fact, a small laundry on a tiny industrial estate, fresh and hopeful, the staff busy and the place buzzing.

Relieved of my sack of clothes, I took a bus to Newtownards and my spirits rose as I passed through villages that were more as I had hoped. Ards, as it is known locally, was a happy town, apparently untouched by the Troubles.

I took a bus on to Bangor, which was bigger and brasher than Ards, to find the Todd Chart Agency, a well run chart and book shop. I looked at the charts and pilot books wondering if I was really going to venture any further. I began to feel slightly seasick just looking at some pink shading on one chart.

Charts and maps have always fascinated me. They are like a secret code to break. The answer to the code can be fully revealed only by visiting the place. It is the nuance and the interpretation that I find most interesting. On a road map you can sometimes pick out where a crossroads is in fact a staggered junction. On a chart there can be a tiny change of depth that reveals danger. More interesting still is converting

73

the model that one creates in the head into an animated design where you can imagine vehicles at the crossroads or tide passing over a rocky ledge.

I was drawn into the books and found myself enthused to adventure onwards. At the same time I knew I had to come up with some better tactics if I was to have the physical ability to continue. A plan began to emerge. It was the realisation that I needed to take smaller steps. I set a target of four-hour passages and studied all the information at hand to see how far I could get that way. I began to plan my next steps; Donaghadee first, then across the North Channel to Portpatrick in Scotland and then round the Rhinns of Galloway to Loch Ryan. I investigated Ballantrae in detail, even trying to get advice from yacht clubs, but it did not look hopeful. The step up from Stranraer to Girvan looked long but perhaps would be possible in five hours. From there it was straightforward all the way to the Crinan because there were marinas, ports and anchorages dotted throughout the region. Even beyond Crinan I could get to Oban without difficulty. The open seas of the Hebrides beyond Mull looked a considerable challenge but I put those to the back of my mind and made Loch Fyne my target.

I selected sufficient publications to take Kippa to Oban. For the most daunting stretch I chose the Admiralty Leisure portfolio which gives fine detail of the Inner Hebrides. I also bought an amusing and informative little book by Sleighthome that began to give me a bit more confidence.

Another aspect of my plan began to form. I had to learn to "heave to" in Kippa. I also had to gain more experience of anchoring. That way I would have more options to stop when I needed to. Strangford Lough was to become my training camp for the next few days to prepare myself for the battles ahead.

Back on board the log was updated; Kippa and I had done 643 miles by this stage of our journey. The next voyage would be all of two miles long! Portaferry to Quoile.

It was a fine evening and the east wind was blowing at least force five. The Lough looked inviting so I raised the jib and off we went, reaching 4.2 knots in open water. As Kippa turned into the Quoile River the wind seemed to funnel down. It was fun dodging the unspoilt little green hillocks that were islands. It reminded me of "Secret Water", the Arthur Ransome book. As I came under the shelter of the islands the wind lost some of its strength and it was a gentle run up into the moorings of the yacht club. I was just about to pick up a mooring when I saw there was a club pontoon with some space, so I tied on there.

The evening sunset was uplifting and I was a little better for having at least got back into Kippa. I did not fancy going back out to sea but at least I had enjoyed some sailing. I settled into my sleeping bag with Scruff, the toy dog, and we pondered the future. His little black eyes stared out and his ears remained pricked up as usual but he said nothing. Kippa lay peacefully with the water caressing her keel. I fell asleep and dreamed of banks and braes.

The next day, 1st of May, the Quoile Sailing Club became active. A Scots lady, who was working on a fine old 50-foot racing yacht, helped me swap sides on the pontoon so as not to be in the way and then I took a long walk up to Killyleagh. I passed a police station made largely of armour and surrounded by high fences that looked as if it was from the set of a movie. In the village I found the Dunferrin Arms, which was more like a grand Irish home than a pub. The dining room served good food and the locals were very amusing. Afterwards I had a peak through the gates of the private castle and then explored the quayside down the hill.

I caught a bus back but the driver flew past my stop and it took a lot of persuasion to get him to stop at all. I ended up being set down so far past the lane I had come along that I was now faced with a trek back; however, the floodplain of the Quoile is a nature reserve and it was all very pretty. Unfortunately the trail had been mapped as an expression of intent, not reality, and I was forced to retrace my steps when confronted by various natural and man-made obstacles. Not sure what to do next, I asked a gentleman and his son, who insisted on driving me round to the yacht club. They dropped me off once we arrived at a shore I recognised and I walked the last stretch along the beach of the Lough. I got chatting to a walker with a dog who turned out to be a member of the sailing club and by the time I was back on Kippa I felt very much part of the scenery.

A gorgeous morning followed with the sun shining and a steady breeze blowing. I set full sail and made my way up to the moorings in front of Killyleagh. As the sun grew hotter the wind became lighter but only on the final stretch did I put the engine on. By sticking to sailing it meant Kippa and I only got as far as Ringhaddy Sound and so I never saw the well-known Down Sailing Club lightship – but I did pick up a mooring in a fine spot where the air and water were crisp and clean.

In the evening Kippa and I explored the eastern side of the Lough before taking up the mooring provided by the ferryman. The next day I flew home from Aldergrove Airport to catch up on paperwork.

26. Portaferry to Donaghadee

Restart

Returning to Belfast, I had a little more time to explore the city. The library was unhelpful and I could not find anywhere to eat but eventually found a modern bar serving fresh, imaginative food, the best of which was a cream tea with tasty soda bread. A Northern Irish speciality, their soda bread is cushion soft inside with a crunchy crust outside. I complimented them on it and they were so pleased with my feedback that when I came to pay the bill they had packed a slice with jam and butter in a little bag for me to take away.

I took the bus to Newtonards, another from there to Portaferry and then hopped on the ferry in order to leave a thank-you bottle of whiskey for the ferryman. On the Strangford side I jumped out and had a look at the quay. I discovered an attractive spot which I might visit with Kippa.

A couple of ferries later I rode back free of charge on the bridge again, a super spot to enjoy the view. Finding no dinghy available to get me across to where Kippa was moored, I made a phone call and knocked on a couple of doors and eventually found someone who would take me across to the yacht. The forecast for the following day was gales so I made plans to stay in the Lough.

In the morning I crossed over with Kippa to Strangford village and tied to the quay. It was nicely sheltered but the wash from the quay worked in and squashed the fenders. With the tide falling away I decided to leave alone and so took a walk through the pretty harbour-side houses and around a little mound to a pine wood that stretched along an inlet where I found a beautiful bay. When the path ran out I followed the main road in search of Castle Ward, the stately home marked on the chart. When I came upon the entrance I wandered up the main drive and then dived amongst the rhododendrons to avoid the natives and tourists. I came out of the undergrowth onto the lawns and was rewarded with a view across the fields and woods to the Lough.

Making my way back to the road, I sought a bus timetable but then decided to try hitching a lift. Only a few vehicles went by before a kindly couple stopped and took me into Downpatrick, right to the cathedral. A rebuilt edifice, it was pleasant and welcoming. I asked if I could use the piano and was allowed to, the first place I had discovered in the British Isles where a cathedral does not stand on ceremony. It was a little out of tune but the tonal effect had a hopeful and light quality. If anyone was listening they soon made themselves scarce.

I had a meal in a simple restaurant, then investigated the High Street and finally took the bus back to Strangford. I had another look around the quay and asked the locals about the options. I settled on the old private quay where they thought I would not be bothered. I studied the Lough bottom, the wall and the rings of the quay and then set up some ropes in advance so that later I could take Kippa round once the tide had risen. Tucked in beside a grass-covered quay, surrounded by the well kept cottages, I was in paradise. Kippa was not obtrusive and seemed very at home, though climbing up the sea wall proved impossible as the boat grounded.

The weather next day was no better so I walked up the road again, ignoring the wind and rain to seek out the Churchtown organic farm shop that I had seen advertised. It was a bit of a trek but well worth it, marvellous South Devon and Aberdeen Angus meat and a wide selection of vegetables for sale. For lunch I chose fresh scones and a raspberry pavlova ice cream which I consumed in their fields, sheltering by a stone wall with ewes and lambs that seemed very content. I huddled in a hollow as best I could while a shower passed over and then dried out when the sun broke through.

I walked back down the hill to Strangford and took up the offer of a cup of tea with Edna and Ted, the couple who had taken me to Downpatrick. They had insisted I should call in and they were pleased to be able to tell me about their family in England. Ted was very interesting about Northern Irish politics, taking a very balanced and wise view from a well informed experience of various committees where he had met people such as Mo Mowlam, the former Northern Ireland Secretary, whom he described as down-to-earth.

Wow, it was tough to leave Strangford the next day. It was really beginning to feel like home. However, the weather forecast was good and the tide was suitable so off we went up the neck of the Lough.

Two other yachts were coming out with the tide as well and a seal popped its head out of the water as if to say goodbye. The tidal stream became rapid and the land slid by. Out into the open sea, Kippa tried her best to sail up the coast. After a while she was becalmed and we began to motor. I set the autopilot and recorded an audio diary for half an hour. The sea became smooth, clouds scudded away southwards, birds flew in formation and the sun began to beat down.

At the end of the morning we passed Ballywalter, a tiny village I had seen from the bus, and the wind began to come from the south. It went from nothing to force four in about half an hour and not long after reached force five so I reefed down one, surfing onwards to Donaghadee.

Within sight of Donaghadee the wind was still building up so I took another reef in to remain in control. I looked for clues to the harbour entrance but could find none so I called on the radio and a lifeboatman from his control room gave me advice as to how to get into the harbour. He advised against entering the marina because he was worried we might hit the rocks guarding the entrance. A lifeboat powered into the harbour, sped past and tied onto the sea wall. I was not sure where to tie up but the friendly crew took my lines and put us by some steps.

During the evening the wind rose to a gale while the rain became incessant. Kippa was chucked about in all directions so through the downpour I struggled to the yacht club around the bay seeking out a bed and breakfast. The club members were very kind and helpful and soon got in touch with a member who ran a B & B. The landlady turned out to be a taxi driver in Belfast, one of only two apparently. She had worked throughout the Troubles but assured me she had not felt too unsafe as a call on the radio would bring taxis from all directions if she was in danger. It was obvious a sodden sailor turning up at 10.30 pm was hardly going to concern someone who took a night shift in the city in her stride.

27. Donaghadee to Troon
Breakdown

A clean and comfortable stay gave me the required rest I needed to tackle the 22 nautical mile crossing to Portpatrick. The rain had cleared and the sun was out with a pleasant breath of wind. Visibility was superb and when Kippa reached the middle of the North Channel which divides Northern Ireland and Scotland, I could see both coasts. The sea was mixed but not rough and it all went well.

Portpatrick is a curious landfall because you can easily see the town from miles out but picking out the leading marks is almost impossible until the last moment. The tide rushes past the entrance and Kippa drifted well off line before I knew what the line was and by the time I was really sure of our position we were almost inside. The final stage is to turn 90 degrees left into the outer harbour and then straight on to the sheltered inner harbour to a very high wall built tall because of the tidal range.

Portpatrick is a pretty little tourist village, nicely kept and sporting a smart putting green and neat houses. I walked up to the main hotel and found it to be a Shearings coach holiday centre. I sneaked in, bought a drink and took a chair so I could enjoy the evening's entertainment of an accordion and dancing. Although the audience were mostly old people, there were a few youngsters too who joined in the dancing from time to time, very expert in their steps on various jigs and reels.

Sunday 13th May was wonderful sailing, which I thoroughly enjoyed (a sure sign of problems round the corner). The harbourmaster at Portpatrick was keen to get rid of yachts on passage because he predicted a change in the weather that would make progress north very difficult. I asked him about the northwards passage and he advised me to stay within one boat's length of the rocks and pick up a tidal eddy, which I did but found that the sailing angle meant Kippa could not stay in as close as he recommended. Fortunately the tide remained favourable a little further out and we made good progress.

At Craig Laggan we anchored in an isolated bay with just one house on the shore. After a snack I did not dally because there were plenty of rocks around and if the weather changed Kippa was vulnerable. We continued on, admiring the Rhinns of Galloway, a very pleasant stretch of coast. When we began to turn the corner of the peninsula the wind was stronger. I reefed the main but still made an exhilarating beat which became a reach of 5.8 knots as we headed east and then a run as we headed south down into Loch Ryan still doing over five knots in what was now a top end force 6 aided by the funnel effect of the loch entrance. The waves built up but they made sense now we were out of the Irish Sea. They came from the direction of the wind making fast sailing enjoyable for a change.

Ferries were coming into the loch as well, some of them fast vessels. For safety we wherried, a big tack from a broad reach to a broad reach, rather than gybed, to maintain control and not get in the way. In Kippa, gybes were inclined to whip the boom over my head even if you have pulled in the controlling mainsheet, whereas I found that a wherry, which involves a gradual turn into the wind, through it and then a gradual bearing away from the wind, was more comfortable in a strong wind. The result was the same, a turn of 60 degrees.

We swept around a sand spit and turned back on ourselves to anchor at The Wig. Unfortunately the shelter was not enough and I was concerned that Kippa might drag anchor. I contacted Stranraer port for local advice and they said I should find more shelter in port. I soon found out that was not correct when I upped anchor and made my way down the loch to find the harbour exposed from the north and the wind stronger. I managed to get Kippa tied onto an old wooden jetty and then stepped off to explore and to call Sarah from a phone box. I carried a mobile phone and at times we communicated that way but overall the landline provided a cheaper, more reliable and safer connection. For internet connection I carried a laptop with a roaming device but here again I found that a library is more convenient because you have a desk and reliable broadband speeds in most cases. For half an hour or longer they are usually free, an exception being Northern Ireland.

The night was not too bad and I slept tolerably. After breakfast I had a look around and found the town to be poor. I had a look in the butcher's and ventured to ask where their meat came from and if any of it might be organic. I got a stare and a very slow shake of the head that told me to get out or I would be the victim of the meat cleaver. A second butcher was more reasonable and agreed to part with a haggis.

When the tide was favourable we set off, tacking against the persistent north wind. It was good sailing and by staying on the eastern edge we got some protection that enabled us to make comfortable progress on smoother water while also keeping away from the ferries. The green and purple hills glistened in the sunlight and I was enjoying myself again, a most ominous sign.

Out from the loch, the wind died and I had to put on the engine. The "False Craig", a hill on the mainland that can mislead mariners, was to starboard and the real Ailsa Craig was north west of us. As we began to explore the Firth of Clyde, rain started to flow in from a new direction. A little wind here and there helped us along but short of our destination, Girvan, Kippa's engine stopped for no apparent reason. I assumed it was fuel. I considered attempting repairs but there was just enough wind to maintain steerage and I could see more developing from the south west. I let the coastguard know my position and asked about entering Girvan under sail. They said it would be impossible to enter the harbour safely under sail but they offered a tow from the lifeboat, which was out on practice anyway. By the time the lifeboat arrived the wind had increased and was pushing Kippa along fast so I took in a reef to remain in control. The call from the lifeboat was calm and supportive; they would follow us in and give Kippa a tow into harbour if I wished. They saw that we were making good progress and suggested we sail on to the harbour since they could tow Kippa no faster than we were going anyway.

Once they had established we were in good shape, sailing confidently, they asked if I minded if they popped off and did some exercises to keep the lads busy. They returned later and offered to put someone on board. I said I could manage, but that if they were doing exercises and wanted to put someone on board, that was fine too.

The lifeboat began to steam closer, motors throbbing, the crew kitted out for action. The structure of the vessel loomed larger and larger over my right shoulder, engines now pulsing like a dragon as the boat surged forward then held back. Its bow ploughed a thick wave of water as closer and closer it came, now almost alongside my starboard beam as we both sped on, Kippa going nearly full speed and the lifeboat trying to match perfectly. I did my best to maintain consistent direction and speed without watching the lifeboat. The steering position of this

Mersey lifeboat was on the starboard side and was out of sight of the port edge of the boat and I wondered what they were going to do. A lifeboatman on the foredeck perched himself on the edge. Even now, I can vividly recall his eyes bulging with a mixture of fear and determination as he leaned away from the lifeboat's front deck while I tried to keep Kippa on a steady course so he would not fall between and be crushed. He waited like a coiled spring, hanging over the side, colleagues ready for action too, and then drew in breath as another crew member relayed to the man on the helm, "Ten metres, four metres, three metres". At three metres he jumped and fell over the guardrail of Kippa, moments later catching a line for the tow. How he managed to clear the guardrails I do not know, for it all happened in a split second.

He bounded into the cockpit and then sat down calmly. I was pleased he did not just take charge but instead introduced himself as John and asked "Anything I can do to help?" It was as if he had dropped in for tea. It was great to have him there and I felt a wave of relief that he was safe. He would have gladly done any task to help but I just gave him the tiller while I got the sails down. We put the fenders on as we were pulled up the channel to the harbour and then there was a bit of a rush as we were swung alongside a motor cruiser owned by the Turnberry Hotel.

A cup of tea did then appear in the lifeboat station while the crew drank McEwans. Everyone, especially John, made me feel very at home; Roddy, harbourmaster and lifeboat mechanic, also introduced himself. Stewart, the coxswain, showed me a picture of the Mersey type lifeboat and explained why he had approached on the blind side of his boat to avoid Kippa's boom. Stewart had that aura of quiet leadership which I find so impressive and inspiring. The crew drank lager and were a good natured lot who had obviously enjoyed their evening exercise.

Next day, Dave, a senior man in the lifeboats, came on board and spent a long time with me guiding me through the process of bleeding the fuel. When we had established fuel was coming through all the filters he was sure the engine would start. It did not. He was mystified. We went right through all the pumps and tubes up to and including the injector, even checking it was producing a mist in the right pattern. It was, but still the engine would not start.

For the next two days I chased the red herring of a fuel fault because that had been what I had been taught to look for and also what everyone advised. I learned that once you have established that fuel is going through to the cylinder correctly you must start to think beyond fuel. Having said that, you might be able to get fuel through manually but that does not mean fuel is getting through when the engine is turning over. Several times Colin, a local marine engineer who was also connected with the lifeboat, did his best to help. We could get the engine running but it would not idle and run properly.

While all this was going on and I was becoming reconciled to more serious trouble, Roddy provided support with his smuggling, geology and history stories. Apparently smugglers came first to Girvan and then the Bog Irish who were escaping the "tattie famine" but best of all was the tale about criminals who were using a trawler to bring drugs from Africa to Britain.

I replaced a hose and had fun visiting Noble's yard, the main boat-builder in the region. They had a reputation for charging over the odds but I found them very helpful with their time and materials. In between attempts to get the engine going I did other jobs such as fixing a leaking window. Noble's came up with stainless steel screws that were a tiny bit wider than the existing screws and these formed the perfect join for the windows to ensure a tight fit. These screws are the answer for windows on a Hunter Horizon 272/273.

Kippa is fitted with a "1GM10" engine from the Yanmar company. Eventually, after Colin had done all he could and I had taken advice from a Yanmar dealer in Cornwall who had been involved in the last service and another in Scotland, it was obvious I would have to sail Kippa up to Troon.

The one last throw of the dice was a man who had serviced the fishing boats in Girvan for many years but had now taken a lorry driving job. He had been away but I had left a message at his home. His name was Andy Marr and when he investigated the lift pump that draws the fuel from the tank to the engine, he discovered how the wear on the lift pump arm had been on one side. He also found that turning the engine over manually was not activating the arm and he suspected this to be the cause of the problem. It may have been an intermittent fault. However, he could still not get the engine to run properly. Either there had been another fault all along or the engine had been damaged in all the efforts to start it. Anyway, the oil level appeared to have risen and so it was concluded that the head gasket had gone. Roddy reckoned this may have been the problem all along and certainly it fitted the symptoms.

It was months later that a different diagnosis was suggested. When I told the story to my car mechanic his conclusion was that the engine was choked up and that fuel was passing the piston rings and this was reducing compression.

The Yanmar dealer had refused to drive down to Girvan so I was obliged to sail to Troon. I was towed out of harbour by a little boat owned by Keith, a fisherman, with Roddy alongside, helping him. Roddy was kitted out with modern clothing and lifejacket and my abiding memory of him is that he was a real professional, knowing when and how to intervene and when best to leave alone.

I sailed Kippa north in light winds, admiring Ailsa Craig, a round granite blob where curling stones come from, and Arran, a grand island that looks as if it could be its own kingdom. On my starboard side I gained a view of the magnificent Turnberry Hotel, which will be dug up in thousands of years and wondered at by golf archaeologists. Past the Turnberry Point the wind increased, bringing dark clouds which blacked out Ailsa Craig, then swept over to the coast and covered it until I lost all visibility. I marked the chart with time and position and continued watching the chartplotter.

Suddenly the display disappeared. I could get it to reappear but it would then shut down again. I switched it off and considered my situation. I made a note of where I was on the paper chart so that I could continue by dead reckoning, using my compass, distance log and the almanac to judge the tide. I called the coastguard to apprise them of my situation.

At sea, one problem tends to lead to another. As we progressed, battery power decreased so low that Kippa's distance log shut down. Along with it the depth sounder went dead. It is by the use of the depth sounder that one is taught how to navigate in fog. Using distance and depth, one can follow a contour of the sea-bed. I was now without both instruments, in fog. For the present I was relying on dead reckoning based on compass and judgement of speed through the water by feel. At this stage I remembered that it was in Western Scotland that local magnetic effects can upset the compass.

I needed to check my calculations so I dug out my back-up GPS set. I pressed the "on" button. Nothing. No response at all.

Perhaps time to call the coastguard again. Except that the radio depended on the main batteries working. There might be a bit of juice left in the engine battery but I decided to keep that in reserve in case I needed to get a reading from the chartplotter. I pulled out the handheld radio and attempted a call. It was working but it was obvious that the signal was not of sufficient strength to reach a coastguard aerial because I received no reply.

I tried to ascertain the problem with the GPS. As well as the rechargeable battery pack, I had a separate battery pack and these could be fitted with conventional batteries. I opened a fresh packet and fitted these. The GPS lit up.

I could be more certain of my position but I was now out of touch with the coastguard via main radio and handheld radio. Once again I had to turn to fresh back-up batteries. I called again, standing high on the deck to improve range and this time the coastguard could just hear me.

I have always been a belt and braces type, hence two anchors, two lengths of chain, spare main radio, handheld radio, two battery sources for all devices, spare sail, water in three kinds of container (I could have been wrecked on an island and lasted months!).

When the fog cleared the wind picked up more strongly and we sped up towards Troon, making careful pilotage amongst off-lying rocks. However, just as we approached the harbour, the south west wind met a north wind and Kippa was becalmed. Suddenly there was not a puff from anywhere, just a bobbing sea. The marina had offered a dinghy to pull me in from the outer harbour anyway so when I let them know why I was delayed they offered to send the dinghy out. I wish they had not bothered. I would have been better anchoring and waiting for an hour for wind. The lads sent out arrived with no lifejackets on and apparently no radio. One man jumped on Kippa and shouted instructions rudely. It was all a stark contrast to the Girvan lifeboat. He then tried to lower the main halyard without putting on the topping lift which holds up the boom, at which point I had to put him straight before there was a serious accident. He then sulked all the way into harbour while his mate in the dinghy smoked at the helm of an engine that smelt to me of petrol.

Kippa and I were dumped in the most remote part of the marina they could find, perhaps as petty revenge and when the marine engineer came on board, he asked, "Why are you here?" as if it were in some way my fault. I just said: "I think they were in a hurry to get home."

Things deteriorated from there on. Kippa was taken out of the water and when the engine's head was taken off there was scoring on the head and block. The engineer said he might be able to get someone to fix the head but it would be three weeks at least. He was even less sure about the block and reckoned the best he could do was to use some kind of liquid metal repair. Overall he could not warrant the work and the message I was getting was new engine or wait a couple of months for it to be fixed.

As it was a 17-year-old engine, I decided I might be throwing good money after bad to attempt to repair it. Also, a long delay would put an end to the dream of circumnavigating Britain in 2007.

Getting a new engine was straightforward; however, persuading the marine engineer to complete the installation required me to be on site continuously, checking on progress all day long.

It was a week of battling before I could finally leave with the new engine. Not feeling confident in the dealer after seeing him struggle with the electrics, I did a test run in Troon outer harbour. I motored Kippa forward, then we motored back. Then I pushed the lever to go forward again but poor Kippa kept going back. The gear was stuck in reverse! I managed to manoeuvre Kippa back into the inner harbour and somehow got safely onto the pontoon. When I found the engineer, all he could say was that I could have put Kippa somewhere more convenient!

New friends, Elaine, Stephen and Andrew, were planning to go out with me that morning but I had to disappoint them. We looked around the boats and left the engineer to fix the problem. When I returned to the boat later, he had gone. I found him though, and he just said some screws had come loose and he had now put on nuts to lock them in place. Might have been as well if he had done this in the first place.

28. Troon to Lochgilphead
Beluga to the rescue

Arran was one of the islands I particularly wanted to visit but with time lost I had to drop it from the schedule. I almost changed my mind as Kippa tacked away from Troon and found herself on a course for Lamlash harbour. Reluctantly I tacked her back towards the north and we sailed on. The sea became rough as the wind funnelled through the gap between the island and the mainland and I was glad when we found some shelter in the lee of the Cumbrae Islands. It was fine sailing with wonderful views of Arran right up to Millport where we moored for a meal before continuing on to Rothesay on Bute. More great sailing, now in calm water but with plenty of wind flying off the mountains. Kippa loved it, leaning very little but doing five knots. It was going too well. I looked down into the cabin to see water sloshing around in the bottom of the boat. Kippa had always been perfectly dry until that point but now I was in for a depressing few weeks, having spent a lot of money on a new engine that had not been fitted correctly. I had chosen the identical engine to replace the old one for the very reason that the installation would be simple, so I was very disappointed to find a new problem had been created.

For safety's sake, I called the coastguard to let them know, then investigated. Nothing was obviously wrong and it was not far to Rothesay so we continued. Had the circumstances been happier I would have enjoyed the final stretch which runs past some fine merchant houses that used to belong to Glaswegian commuters from the height of Empire. Entering the harbour was made easy with the help of a couple of people alerted by the coastguard who ensured that Kippa had a clear space to be safely tied up.

I investigated the leak and found water and oil below the engine as well as the bilge pump unattached. It was with a heavy heart that I began the mopping up. Little did I know that the daily clean-up would become a regular part of my routine for weeks to come. I considered returning to Troon but dismissed the idea. There would be nothing to gain from an installer who did not seem to care about my safety. All that would happen is that time would be lost.

The next day I decided to explore the island, which is owned by the Marquess of Bute. Apparently he owns land in Spain and elsewhere too. The family married into money several times and built Mount Stuart, a Gothic house that is vast and looks like Hogwarts. Breathtaking when you first see it, rather less so as you get up close and realise that it is slightly naff. Inside, too, reminded me of a Ford Escort with dice on the mirror and nodding dog on the parcel shelf. One can imagine pearls and medallions being worn by the inhabitants of this home that was more quirky than stately. We were told by the guide that the family are Protestant turned Catholic, with mysticism and various cults mixed in, which explained the astrological stained glass as well as the constellations made of silver and crystal stuck on the ceiling. There was a chapel, modelled on Zaragoza's cathedral, made of sandstone lined with marble which only served to create a Formica-on-plywood effect.

On the other hand, the garden was full of wonderful trees and shrubs, while the lawn in front of the house was simple and serene, looking down over the sea loch. Garden only ticket is the way to go because one could spend the whole day wandering around the 300 acres. The modern visitor centre is a more pleasing architectural effort, using wood to blend in with the woodland environment and wide expanses of glass to let you appreciate the views.

On Saturday 26th May a brisk north easterly was blowing right into the harbour of Rothesay. Kippa and I tacked out and then headed north west up the East Kyle. The fine scenery was enhanced by pretty little houses, the occasional jetty and mooring. The Burnt Isles provided an interesting chicane amongst the birds with the wind dropping as the mountains grew. Where the East Kyle meets the West Kyle there is a tiny anchorage behind an island called Caladh Harbour. Had there been more wind we would have sailed through but instead we carried the tide and headed south. The sun shone and we drifted along contentedly past Tighnabruaich amongst a few other yachts out for the weekend. The wind picked up a little and fed in from the west while I enjoyed a marvellous view of the mountains on the Isle of Arran, now viewed from the north. It looked a forbidding place and I wished I had time to go across and land.

In these idyllic conditions I made a decision that nearly cost us dear. I was looking for a place to stop for lunch and saw an anchorage marked on the west side of the West Kyle, nicely sheltered. I thought to myself that if the wind direction swung to the north or south it would still be safe. There were no rocks marked so we went in close and I dropped anchor. I had a bite and settled down for a short rest.

An hour passed and I noticed the wind had changed so I came on deck. It was blowing more strongly now but much worse than that, it had swung round 180 degress and was now an easterly. Before I could get the engine on or a sail up it was force five and Kippa was straining on the anchor chain. The tide should have been at its lowest but it still seemed to be falling. At that moment Kippa started to ground. I looked over the side. Now I could see something that had been invisible before. There was a cluster of small rocks and they were only ten metres away. In one sense it was good that I had grounded because the easterly was trying to turn Kippa onto them.

I tried to pull on the anchor chain. I ran the engine. It was no good. Kippa floated momentarily and then bounced onto the sea-bed again. I was in a precarious situation but the danger could get worse. I checked the tide tables. I did calculations for three local spots but it was obvious none of the predictions was correct for today. Local or climatic conditions were overriding. I peered down at the rocks again. They were about two or three metres in width and height. And quite jagged. I looked around and began to consider calling for help. I was reluctant to call the coastguard, having troubled them twice recently. The wind was now bringing a cold heavy rain with it too, just to make things more miserable.

I looked around and saw that a much bigger yacht had followed me into the anchorage. It had anchored further out and I assumed it was safe. With binoculars I could read the name of the boat, appropriately called Beluga, and called them for help. There was a delay before they answered. When they did, I discovered they too had been in bother and said they had just got off in time with only 20 centimetres below their keel. Something I discovered during our attempts to communicate was that channel six was not a good choice for a working channel. It was too easily confused with channel 16, the distress channel.

Now clear of danger, Beluga's skipper came across with a line in his dinghy, while the first mate, his wife, tried to stay on station in safe depth. The wind blew strongly and he could not get close enough. It was a Thunderbirds scenario. I was in trouble and just out of reach of help. We tried more line but it was no good. He could get to me but he could not then get the line to Beluga. Meanwhile his wife was worrying about grounding their boat, understandably so as by now I realised they had two children on board, who were being very good and staying below. Neil, the skipper, did not give up and offered me anchor, chain and any help. I was worried that I could get them into trouble and decided to keep battling on my own to get off. The weather improved a little after the tide turned and I was beginning to sense Kippa was ready to float at any minute. Fortunately the wind had backed a little to north east and dropped in strength back to a force four.

With the skipper back on board, Beluga remained on station and would not leave the area with me still floundering. Finally Kippa floated and immediately I pulled on the anchor chain with all my strength. I had to get her forward before she swung onto the rocks. I could not look and see how close we were, I just kept hauling and hoping.

The chain went tight and I knew we were now close to the anchor. I gave a final tug and the anchor came out. I quickly got the remaining chain on board and the anchor into the locker, rushing back into the cockpit to drive Kippa into deep water. We just made it and Beluga waved. The whole family were on deck now to cheer us on. We spoke on the radio. I would have liked to follow them but they were going in the other direction and I wanted to press on to a safe marina to do yet more cleaning up, but I was sorry to say goodbye. Beluga was a special boat and stuck to it to the very end, prepared to do what it took to save Kippa. The boys on Beluga gave a friendly wave and I waved back, ignoring a tear in my eye. Of all the boats that helped us, Beluga was particularly special because she was such a classy yacht of a type you rarely see where style and quality combined, yet the skipper put himself out for us in a completely selfless way. What had also come across was that Neil had good sense, good seamanship and a quiet and gentle way that oozed support and encouragement. Yet in some ways, in must have been his wife who suffered most that day. She had been put in charge of Beluga, had to look after the children, had seen her husband rowing away to danger, struggling with ropes to a stupid little yacht ruining her day. Poor little Kippa and her skipper were very forlorn in comparison, but we survived another day and another adventure.

That evening, after more heavy showers, wind coming and going from all directions, a sunset began and the clouds took on that pale blue of icing on a wedding cake which is so Hebridean. I felt Mull and Skye were beckoning. We stopped the night in Portavadie, a new marina, opposite East Loch Tarbert.

The rain came pouring down again but we were sheltered from the wind and although there were only basic facilities I was comfortable. The wind abated during the night and when I arose early there was hardly a breath. I had breakfast and visited the Portacabin loos. Exploring up amongst the gorse above the marina I felt a breeze coming down from the north. I decided not to use the engine and instead set sail from the pontoon. I have always liked sailing in or out of a marina, so long as it is reasonably safe and this was a perfect opportunity. Kippa slipped along by the shore and out through the gap in the sea walls. The wind was moderate as we came out from the shelter. Avoiding the fish farm, we reached across the loch to get a view of East Loch Tarbert, one of the Scottish jewels but filled with yachts that had been taking part in an important racing series. We did not stop but sailed right into and out of the harbour. It was then a beat up Loch Fyne to Ardrishaig where you enter the Crinan Canal. In the basin was a marvellous old wooden boat with a plastic shell added later. The owner was a tall, gawky character, part gent, perhaps part anarchist, an offbeat and original. He and his crew came alongside Kippa and I was worried we would be crushed by this heavy, stubby ship with its toerail that looked like battlements. However, the rickety old topsides and ancient ropes, not to mention the old Ford diesel pounding away below, became safely moored alongside the quay behind Kippa. This fishing boat turned pleasure cruiser could easily be the basis of a cartoon character and certainly she had been on some adventures, according to the crew.

After a cup of tea, Kippa and I progressed through locks up to Lochgilphead, where we stopped for the night and a clean of the bilges, as usual.

29. Lochgilphead to Arisaig
A sprig of heather

The Crinan Canal starts from Loch Fyne, first passing Lochgilphead, a humble town in a fine setting overlooking its own little inlet of Loch Fyne called Loch Gilp, which is blessed with a grocer selling organic products as well as a fine foods delicatessen and baker. On the up-slope the canal is pleasant but not spectacular, but as you descend, the scenery lights up gloriously. At Cairnbaan, near the summit, I met up with Alan and Donald, tugmen from Lochalsh who had been racing at East Loch Tarbert. We descended the locks together, which made for good progress, and eased the burden being single-handed. Old oak woods became marshy and when Crinan Bay opened out there was a new and exciting landscape to behold. The bay is strewn with islands and islets, little hills are dotted with the occasional farmhouse. There are no radio masts, no wind generators, nothing to suggest which century you are in.

We came to Crinan Basin, one of the best places in Britain to stop. Surrounded by such natural beauty, I felt a fraud to take my laptop up the hill to get a connection and sit incongruously on the soft heather amongst ancient woodlands. A family of walkers came by and could not help but laugh to see me there collecting e-mails. In the distance were the wild Hebrides where new technology seems very out of place.

Alan and Donald came on board to share my Jura whisky and they talked in their lilting accents, Donald's being a particularly soft musical tone that is Skye but sounds rather Irish.

Crinan Basin is a convenient port, with a friendly boat repairer and chandlery, helpful waterways staff, great views and excellent shelter. Next day, though, we had to leave. The wind was good, even if there were clouds and showers, and Kippa and I were off into the wilder side of Kintyre, away from the hordes and townies of the Firth of Clyde and in amongst the evocative scenery. Strong tides had returned now that we were subject to the Atlantic currents and we shot through the gaps between headlands, such as Dorus Mor, and surged through inter-island channels, like the Shuna Sound. This was the best sailing yet: fast but still comfortable with no room for seas to build up.

I chose Ardinamir, between Luing and Torsay, an anchorage with a tiny entrance, and was blessed with good luck. I had failed to read the pilot book sufficiently carefully and misinterpreted the chart. This was pointed out to me by the skipper of an interesting craft on a double anchor. Fate had led me to the best sailors I had seen on the trip so far – Phil and Gill. These people were not just experienced, they were deeply knowledgeable as a consequence of pushing themselves to new achievements. Their vessel was a trimaran, a Farrier 27, which is a decidedly quick boat that does eight knots with ease and 12 knots if you press on. They understood its limitations too: heavy weather, beating against a force six and above, and grounding on anything but soft sand because of the delicate hull. However with a lifting centreboard they had a one foot draft. With two anchors set at right angles, one the traditional fisherman's type, they could settle themselves beyond everyone else in an inlet and swing in a tiny circle as if on a mooring. It turned out that they also owned a Falmouth workboat, a traditional gaff rigged craft, and have in the past owned a 35-foot yacht that they sailed to the Faeroes and back.

Phil and Gill gave an excellent demonstration of the speed possible with a lightweight construction and how a shallow draft compensates for the lack of strength. Through the excitement of Cuan Sound where the tide charges past the tiny settlements, Kippa and I followed them up to the popular anchorage of Puilladobhran which had been recommended to me by Tony, a friend of Martyn, during a brief but enjoyable stay with his family near Dumfries.

I rowed to shore and walked the path to the Tigh an Truish Inn to enjoy good food with them by Clachan Bridge, which was built with a massive arch to allow large vessels to pass underneath. Returning with a little whisky and beer inside, I had to concentrate on not falling in on my way back to Kippa in the dinghy. I can imagine how it is all too easy to be drowned after a night out if you overdo it.

After a very peaceful stay, the weather sounded doubtful so I waited to see if others ventured out. They did, and it turned out to be another good sail up to Kerrera. I planned only a short stop but was invited to their open day and had a great time eating up the last of the scallops, salmon and oysters. I missed seeing the flying boat take off but then with such fresh local food to guzzle, it was an understandable omission.

Oban I found uninspiring, slightly rip-off, lacking authenticity, so Kippa and I pressed on to Loch Aline, another tranquil setting.

I awoke at 2.30 am and, knowing there would be a favourable tide, thought I might get up. At 3 am I did and was rewarded with the finest day of sailing in my life.

The sunrise coloured the clouds at 4 am as we passed Tobermory. A following wind of variable strength, but a positive tide encouraged me to continue. As we came out of the Sound of Mull, Coll and Tiree appeared. Coll was a small dark sierra and Tiree almost nothing, a quiet introduction to one of the finest views you can appreciate from a yacht. As we reached Ardnamurchan Point, with trepidation following reports of a bad tidal race, the water remained calm so we closed into shore. As we did so, the wind grew in strength and Kippa surfed up to maximum speed with Rolly, the dinghy, hanging on behind. Finally the Small Isles appeared with Rum as their backdrop. I was enjoying the speed so much I could not bring myself to reef down and instead took full advantage to get Kippa into Sanna Bay, a difficult anchorage with a tiny community, protected by rocks and reefs. The katabatic wind whistled down the slopes and I did my best to rest while I waited for the tide to turn.

The sun was out and the sky full of Simpson clouds (cumulus) but to be safe I set in two reefs. That gave Kippa reasonable speed until the katabatic effect wore off and then onshore sea breezes cancelled out the south easterly. No matter, Kippa was now sailing with full rig, past Muck and then Eigg, with its cliffs and crofts. All the time Rum stood proud and aloof in the distance until a strip of land, much further away, appeared. It was Skye with the outline of the Cuillin Hills, pointing up from the horizon.

Arisaig was our destination, a tricky entrance amongst rocks, but a rewarding one. A white painted rock is the first mark to identify but it looks like a house from afar. It was the poles marking rocks that were the first marks I could positively identify and from there I could see a grey house. As you turn in the channel there is a road you use as a transit. The port and starboard poles are perched on rocks and you have to stay mid channel to avoid catastrophe. Once we were into the loch the south easterly returned with full force and Kippa was able to sail at full speed to the final moorings.

A passage of 15 hours with a four-hour break and gales forecast meant that the first accommodation I could find, Arisaig Hotel, was an easy option, especially with an en- suite bath, a double room, a sea view, a Drawing Room (not a lounge), and big, old leather chairs, all for £45 a night.

Had I realised that we had the right, I would have picked a sprig of heather for Kippa's bow now that we had passed Ardnamurchan Point, the most westerly point of mainland Britain. Only later did I learn of the tradition from my friend Ian Boyce, who had encouraged me all the way along the trip by e-mail.

30. The Small Isles

Island life

Kippa was still leaking water and I considered seeking help locally but saw that expertise and facilities in Arisaig were limited. This was probably my last chance to decide whether to go round the top of Scotland or not. I had plans to do so, with advice from Tony who knew the area well. It had been a long-held ambition to revisit Lochinver and Stornoway where my parents had taken us on holiday as children.

My mind was made up by an unexpected turn of events. On the first morning in the hotel I thought it time to do some exercises, making the most of the space. I did some gentle yoga and a couple of press-ups as the next stage of rehabilitating my shoulder, which I had damaged in a bicycle accident in January.

Then I took a walk through the woods to a bay where some small yachts lay sheltered on moorings. On the way back I realised I was in bother. By the next day I was in considerable pain.

Ashley had confirmed he was coming on the sleeper to Arisaig the next day and here I was with a shoulder that was becoming a liability. On the Monday morning I had no choice but to find a doctor. Fortunately there is a smart modern surgery in the village and a kind young doctor working there. He explained the options and suggested I should take painkillers and make my way to a physiotherapist in Fort William. The problem was that Ashley was on his way and I could not let him down. I recalled vividly the hell I put Keith and Morris through and was determined that Ashley should not suffer a similar fate.

The gales had blown all weekend bringing torrential rain but now the sun was out and the wind was feathering down from the north. It was at this point I sadly had to accept defeat. I really did not feel it safe to take Ashley northwards. Kippa with a leak that was still not identified and with a frozen shoulder limiting my movement, we would be in serious trouble if something else went wrong.

I sat at a little café table about to walk up to the station to meet Ashley when he appeared unexpectedly. I must have misread the timetable but he did not seem to mind and we had a snack in the warm sunshine and caught up on our news. As ever, he was in good spirits and that lifted my mood. When the tide came up, we went in a dinghy to collect Kippa from a mooring. Then we set off for the island of Eigg.

Ashley's first voyage was ideal. The islands looked their best in the evening light and the wind made for a steady sail, strong enough to require a reef but never uncomfortable. Into the new harbour at Eigg we tied up to the quay next to a yacht with a friendly local couple aboard.

Next day, while Ashley chatted to the neighbours, I went for a walk on the south side of the island to enjoy views of Muck and to discover a wee croft now used as a holiday home. When I came back it turned out that Ashley had been given a tour of the island and had nearly been persuaded to stay permanently. He had fallen for Eigg, which has about 74 inhabitants and became "independent" in 1997. Previously it had been owned by a German who hardly even visited. Now it was owned by the people living there.

We made the short hop to Muck and anchored in the harbour of Port Mor. We took a walk together to the north of the island where Ashley chose to stop and soak up the wonderful views. I carried on walking to see more of the island. When we met up again later, Ashley had hit the jackpot again. From his viewpoint on a hillock he had seen a family of seals come into a little bay. My walk had been less noteworthy but nevertheless I found serenity in the isolated rolling fields and empty coves.

For supper we went to the gift shop where we had booked a table. They told us that they had already got a booking for a group of six and there would only be leftovers, but hey, what a great set of leftovers they turned out to be! The two ladies who ran the place used big old saucepans to create wholesome tasty dishes. Three courses and we were completely stuffed.

Wednesday brought a more favourable northerly wind of force four, touching five. There was sun and great visibility. Ashley caught a glimpse of a minke whale and although we chased groups of seabirds we did not find it again.

We looked wistfully south to Coll and Tiree, knowing that Iona was beyond, but I again settled for the safe option and turned Kippa towards the Sound of Mull.

As we ran fast before the wind the mainsail pushed the lazy jacks, the strings to help lower sails neatly, until they got caught between the spreader and the shrouds, which hold up the mast. Ashley was growing in confidence with his helming so he steered Kippa into Kilchoan so we could moor temporarily while we sorted out the problem. In no time at all we were on our way again, sailing into Loch Sunart, which cuts deep into the mainland. Oronsay Island protects the south side of the loch and encloses a body of water called Loch Drumbuie. It is a well known anchorage and we had four or five yachts for company.

Ever the adventurous type, Ashley was keen for us to make camp on Oronsay so we rowed across with a couple of potatoes and the kettle. We cut through the undergrowth and found signs of human habitation. However, the crofts had long been deserted and only walls were left. We squished through marshy bogs, scratched through brambles and explored high and low. We settled on higher ground where the sun would still shine, in the hope that this would keep off the midges. We gathered firewood and Ashley did his Ray Mears imitation, creating a beautiful little oven of a fire. It was a while before the potatoes were cooked, but they were delicious. We drank tea and munched seed toast and butter. Kippa's shiny kettle was blackened but Ashley assured me that this was its christening. Ashley told tales of Vladivostok, jellyfish and forests until the midges started to bite and we made our way back to the dinghy to row home to Kippa.

A gentle westerly was feeding into the loch the following morning so we tacked out, getting perilously close to rocks in the very narrow entrance. The water was clean and the chart was detailed and here I felt confident we were safe. Out in Loch Sunart it was slow going but once we turned south west we had the wind coming across our rear quarters. To pick up more speed I dug out the big colourful scooper sail and this pulled Kippa along at a very respectable rate. We did our best to avoid having to gybe but eventually we were caught on a run and had to take the scooper down to be able to manoeuvre. We passed Loch Aline and stopped at a peaceful anchorage by a ruined castle. We were tired but content. Ashley had a kip while I picked up e-mails on the laptop and then we were off again to Kerrera. The wind died and we were forced to motor the final stage to the marina.

Ashley had a look around Kerrera while I had someone try and identify the leak. He was surprised to see how poorly the installation had been done and did various jobs such as replacing the exhaust pipe, double clipping hoses and so on. He seemed a competent man and I was hoping that at last I might be getting on top of the problem.

This left me wondering if perhaps I could go round the top of Scotland after all. My shoulder was getting better and I was reducing the dose of painkillers. I looked carefully at the forecast for the coming week and was not encouraged. Winds from the north and unsettled weather were not what I had hoped for in June. I considered the timings. I was certainly behind schedule. The following morning I checked for leaks. There was still some water coming in. Not much, but enough to set aside any hope of attempting Cape Wrath and the Pentland Firth.

Ashley had enjoyed his week with me and I was delighted he had. There had been no mishaps of any consequence, he had done lots of the sailing and we had spent a relaxing week enjoying the islands. If only the rest of the trip could have been the same. Unfortunately the summer of 2007 was over and from then on the weather was cold and miserable for many weeks. Wind whistled down from the north and I was glad not to be caught on the exposed northern coast in such an awful June.

31. Oban to Inverness
Limping along

After Ashley left us in Oban, Kippa and I progressed to Loch Creran and then to Ballachulish and Glencoe. The Lynn of Lorn was pleasant sailing and Loch Creran was a quiet backwater.

Gaining confidence, I sailed fast under the bridge at Ballachulish and took up a space on the pontoon at Lochaber Watersports. There was a break in the clouds so I walked up the hillside to get a view of the loch. The next day I chose to leave a little early, taking the ebb tide out of Loch Leven and then turning north, where I had hoped the tide would be slack. However, it was still flowing out and with wind also against us we were forced to motorsail in order to make the tacks as we approached the strait called Corran Narrows.

A big old yacht coming south shot past us with tide and wind in its favour. We battled on and managed to squeeze through the Corran Narrows. Pleased with myself, I now had six hours of tide to carry us up to Fort William. It was not to be. I glanced down below and saw that poor Kippa had become more flooded than ever before. I switched off the engine and pumped the bilge pump but discovered it was useless. I had to stop and investigate the problem. My nearest refuge was back south, so I sailed back through the narrows and turned into the sheltered bay. I was glad to have purchased an extra length of chain. I sailed up to the beach as close as I dared but still there was depth of 10 metres close in. The extra chain meant I could get Kippa safe on a depth to chain length multiple of 4.8. It is recommended to be at least three times chain length to the depth of water so at 4.8 I felt reasonably safe.

Once anchored securely I emptied out the boat by sponge and bucket. Investigating, I wondered if Oban had incorrectly clipped the stern gland. By now it was evening and I was coming to the conclusion that the stern gland must be the problem. I called Dave, the previous owner, who advised me how to put things back the way they should be. This did stem the flood but I was not sure the problem was solved. Dave's advice suggested I needed to adjust a collar that seats against a bellows but for this I needed an Allen key which I did not carry. I got some rest for a few hours and then in the middle of the night I was back to cleaning up and investigating the leak. I got the bilges completely dry and then searched for a drop. It was very difficult to identify the source of the problem but gradually I was coming to the conclusion that it had to be the stern gland.

During the early morning I racked my brains for a solution and by breakfast time decided to see if Lochaber Watersports at Ballachulish might have a key. I gave them a call about 9 am and we agreed to meet at another anchorage at Onich in the entrance to Loch Leven. This would enable me to avoid losing another day and would be easy for them to reach by launch. I was indeed fortunate that this was a very well organised little sailing school. The owner, Alex, came out in a fast rib to lend me his key, which was very decent of him. He was impressively attired with helmet and safety gear.

After I had got the collar of the stern gland in a better position, Kippa and I pressed on, back through the Corran Narrows. I was feeling very low at this stage. It was obvious things were not right. The only good thing was that my shoulder had eased and was no more than uncomfortable.

We passed Fort William and entered the Caledonian Canal at Corpach. The leak was not as bad as it had been but there was still some water seeping in. The basin at Corpach had an interesting mixture of ships and the odd yacht. I was now focused on reaching Inverness, where I had heard Caley Marine would be the best place in the North of Scotland to sort Kippa out. Before we could get there we had to traverse Loch Lochy, Loch Oich and Loch Ness, as well as various locks. It was at this very opportune moment that a mother ship appeared in the shape of a Hallberg Rassy 36 called Atherina (named after a small Greek fish and therefore Kippa-related.) The owner and crew were very kind and guided me along, even strapping Kippa alongside in the locks. Dick was an ideal character for my predicament. He is a man of considerable experience, self-confidence and skill so I was very comfortable to follow his guidance. He could tell I was not happy about the engine. A rattle had developed and the engine battery did not seem to be doing its job properly. The leak had improved but it was still there.

Through the locks, Dick tied Kippa to Atherina and then drove us through as a raft alongside a barge. He coped with the help of his wife, Ange, and their crew, who were equally kind and friendly. We sailed up Loch Lochy, stopped the night at Laggan and then Fort Augustus. I had a chat with a fellow circumnavigator, the owner of Popstar, and then a very pleasant evening aboard Atherina.

The following day the wind still whistled down from the north and it was again low cloud or rain most of the way. At Fort Augustus Kippa had a very tricky exit with the wind blowing us into a tight corner. I tried a stern spring but there was not sufficient leverage. I had to work out how to spring off from the bow without running into Atherina in front but also not getting blown into Popstar, behind. I also had to work out how to avoid a rope getting caught in the propeller. I compromised with just sufficient rope at the bow to spring the stern away from the pontoon but not so much that it would draggle too long. It required me to jump back into the cockpit at the right moment and confidently drive backwards. This I managed but in doing so I was running out of space, with boats on one side and rocks on the other and the wind pushing Kippa back. I went into forward and as soon as I had a little space, got the bow rope in and the fenders out of the way. Safely into open water, I decided to keep engine on and bash through Loch Ness. Sailing would take a long time and I was worried that the engine might not restart, the battery had become so weak. It was a cold, wet, miserable voyage, below depressing dark cloud.

Just as we reached Inverness, Atherina came past. Dick had been quietly following us at a discreet distance, ready to help out if we got into trouble. I was relieved to get to Caley Marine because Kippa was in a sorry state. However, I mused whether my experience of marine engineers at Troon and Oban might be repeated. My predicament was put into perspective by a yacht to which Kippa was rafted. With mast down and bits scattered all around the deck, the strong Swedish boat had quite a story to tell. The skipper had been with a friend and a family near Iona when they started to sink. The lifeboat had got to them just in time but the engine and all the equipment had been ruined, all because two pipes that drain the cockpit had corroded at an elbow, allowing water to siphon in. The noteworthy part of their story was that the boat had begun sinking much faster when the crew got into the cockpit in preparation for launching the liferaft. The skipper had not begun to appreciate the cause of the leak until the lifeboat had taken off most of the people; they had pumped out the water and discovered back at Oban that the leak stopped when the weight of the some was reduced.

Caley Marine were well organised, friendly and professional. The foreman immediately came on board and got stuck into seeing what could be done. It was agreed that Kippa had to be lifted out of the water in order to resolve the problems.

£1000 later, Kippa was afloat with a new stern gland, new battery and fuel pipe. While the work was being done I went home on the sleeper and caught up with business and domestic paperwork.

32. Inverness to Cromarty

Fading Popstar

On the West Coast of Scotland people would say: "Why do you want to go to the East Coast, there is nothing there?" I was soon to discover how wrong they were. Indeed, two of the most congenial and interesting villages in Scotland are Cromarty and Findhorn.

With a shocking bill settled, Kippa and I dropped down through the Muirtown locks and took up a position on a lower pontoon. With no water available close by, I was advised to use the fire hose. The water from it came out yellow so I tried a standpipe by the office and that ran clean. Still smarting from the cost of putting right something that should never have been wrong, I then found I was paying £9 to clean my laundry without it getting dry. Nevertheless, the staff were pleasant so I topped up with diesel. As I returned to the pontoon Popstar appeared. I invited the skipper on board because he was keen to look at my charts and almanac. I discovered his almanac was a mere 20 years out of date and he had no chart, though he did plan to buy one for the next stage. We made our way out through the locks with two trawlers and then began to sail in tandem, Popstar outsailing Kippa, which I put down to the weight we were carrying – of charts, pilot books and almanacs, for example.

Calculating the tide, I wanted to press on and, finding ourselves making hardly any progress against the wind, I put on the motor. Popstar continued to sail and soon dropped behind. Over the radio Popstar complained so I switched off and sailed some more, but it was no good so we agreed to motor.

As Kippa pulled further ahead, though by no means rushing, I kept in radio contact with Popstar. The quality of signal from her had always been weak but now it began to break up as well. I was in a quandary because the light was fading and I did not want to enter

Cromarty, a tiny and difficult harbour, in pitch black at the wrong state of tide. I felt a cad but I pressed on. For a long time I could see Popstar in the distance but eventually she was out of sight. When Kippa reached Cromarty Firth I radioed again, told him where we were and gave him a waypoint and directions.

There was still a little light in the sky and I got a pleasant view of the village. The harbour was no problem to find but the entrance looked very tight. I prepared warps and fenders and went in. I was confronted with a tiny harbour and one pontoon down the middle. It required a snap decision. Kippa and I passed the end of the pontoon and turned into the south side. Fortunately a Dufour 37, with Mike, the skipper, and two trainees, helped us to come alongside.

Supper on board their smart yacht was offered and gladly accepted. Haggis, neaps and tatties were on the menu and very good they were too. I liked Mike immediately. Friendly, straightforward and worldly-wise. The acceptable red wine and fresh fruit salad probably had an influence.

However, I could not relax until Popstar appeared. I talked over the situation with Mike and his crew and decided I would call the coast-guard, which I did from his radio. The coastguard tried to raise Popstar but without success at first. When eventually they did get through they were able to report that the radio signal was very broken nevertheless, Popstar was on her way.

In darkness, Popstar appeared but then went past the harbour entrance. We heard her skipper call the harbourmaster and ask for the bridge to be opened. There is no harbourmaster and the bridge is fixed so I called the skipper and advised him where the entrance was. Mike was getting concerned because he knew that Popstar was amongst shallows on a falling tide. With some persuasion, Popstar reluctantly came into the harbour through the correct entrance and tied up. Mike took him a plate of food, realising that it might be best if I kept out of the way. Anyway, in the morning Popstar had vanished.

Cromarty is an architectural delight. Fine houses, some grand, some simple, neatly weaved along a beach, nestling beside the deep and historic Cromarty Firth. Cromarty lies in a corner of the Black Isle, which looked inviting from the sea even in low cloud. The Firth is full of marine life, including dolphins, though I saw only the many and varied seabirds. In the harbour there are sand eels and sea trout.

I did a bit of drawing in the town and had a scone in a bookshop. A feature of the North East of Scotland is that bookshops have a café attached. Inverness has one of the finest, Leakeys, a place reminiscent of a converted church with a balcony upper floor and a café in the roof. Amongst the books and knick-knacks by the window of this multi-functional retail outlet in Cromarty there was a fascinating pink and grey painting. Not completely realistic, it was as if it had been painted by someone who could not do perspective. However, I was not fooled. The slightly abstract style was wonderful, its apparent childish naivety was subtle. I asked the proprietor what it cost, hoping he might say £300 or something of that order. Surely this was just a local artist who was very good and undiscovered. Not a bit of it. This was an A.N. Hardie and the price was £1,500. (He was a local artist who died in 1987.) I could not quibble. It was worth every penny, though beyond my price range. I left feeling deflated by the disappointment that he was discovered but elated that I had now discovered him too.

The post office and police station and several other houses were architectural gems. The amiable people in the harbour were very genuine and I left wanting to return to this corner of Britain.

33. Cromarty to Findhorn
Breaker

The next passage was a straight route across to Findhorn Bay. I allowed plenty of time so that we could sail and avoid using the motor if the wind died. We found ourselves tacking in Cromarty Firth getting a close-up view of the cliffs and birds. The sea was slight or moderate and I felt a little more confident, even though there was still a very slight leak.

It was all going too well again but this time I was expecting trouble because I realised that the entrance to Findhorn could be dangerous. I had studied the almanac, pilot book, chart and chartplotter. I had also taken local advice at Cromarty, however, when I found the fairway buoy it did not seem to be where it was charted. Certainly the first red and green buoys were in a strange spot in comparison. Their colours, red and green, were clear enough so we went through between them. We came out from the second set (which were not charted as a pair) and sought the next sign of the channel. All I could see was a tide gauge and poles, but they were nondescript. Should I take them to port or starboard? I called on a local radio channel to see if anyone might be listening. No response, so I called on the open channel, 16, but again no response except the coastguard asking if I was all right. I explained the problem and they went away to seek help. I dithered and we found ourselves amongst breakers between the buoys and the tide gauge. Kippa grounded momentarily with a large wave under her hull but was immediately afloat again. By the time the second wave hit I was already quickly turning Kippa, using sail and motor to attempt to drive us off. Kippa bounced a second time, stopping and then being swung to one side as a wave brought us up. The third breaker was big and its foam crashed over the deck. We were lifted by it and swept along, to be dumped seconds later.

Trying to remain calm, I judged how much throttle to apply to get us out of trouble but not damage the propeller as sand was being churned up by the waves. As Kippa lifted on the next swell I gave a moderate burst of power and we struggled a short way and touched again, but more lightly. Another quick shove on the rise and we were into deeper water by the time a larger breaker came through that might have damaged the keel bolts. I did not let the scenario of losing keel go through my mind because then the rudder would be lost and we would be destined to be beached like a stricken whale. Instead, I found myself carefully edging Kippa back to where I could be sure of deep water between the red and green buoys. The coastguard were getting worried about us and, when I tried to reassure them we were in safe water, the cockpit microphone jammed on transmit so I switched off so as not to block the distress channel for other people. I grabbed the handheld, which I knew was fully charged up, and got through. The Aberdeen coastguard were brilliant and had come up with a solution in no time at all. They had hunted for local help and found the owner of the boat-yard – except he was not at the boatyard, he was at a petrol station some miles away from Findhorn – but he had a mobile phone with him and they had tracked him down. I was patched through to Simon (not Danno at "Hawaii 50" but good enough for me) and he guided me in by radio: "Two boat lengths to the west of the poles."

"There are breakers on both sides of the poles," I replied.

"You are safe midway between the poles and the beach" and then just as he said to the coastguard who were listening in, "He will be OK from here because the channel becomes clear...", the connection was lost and I could not receive from Simon or the coastguard.

However, he was correct and we were soon safe inside the glorious expanse of water with the village of Findhorn stretching into the distance along a beautiful beach.

The haven was a magical scene of children playing with not a care in the world. People were a bit surprised to see Kippa but were pleased to receive an explorer on a mission. The yacht club members were most welcoming and explained how and where I had grounded and were not in the least surprised at my predicament. It was par for the course.

It is interesting how a local yachtsman's knowledge extends only a very short way. At Cromarty hardly anyone knew the entrance to Find-horn and the man who did was out of date. And here at Findhorn they seemed confused about compass direction (one gentleman pointed to north and, on double checking, it was northeast) and even their interpretation of tide times did not tally with the almanac – but it hardly mattered because they were the friendliest bunch yet encountered in Britain. Bill offered a sail in his Albacore, a wooden dinghy, and then a man called Peter came along to see who I was. Realising I had come some way, he immediately offered me the use of the washing machine and dryer at his holiday home.

On Saturday, Bill and I had a super set of three races and he let me helm in one of them despite having only just met me, generosity one would rarely see down south. The cold rain poured down all through the racing so I was glad of a warm shower at the end – even though it had been fun of a sort.

The weather turned from bad to worse; rain and drizzle with strong winds had become high gales. I was beginnning to get behind my schedule even though I had cut the corner and avoided the worst of the weather along the North Coast of Scotland. I walked down to the Find-horn Foundation, a settlement of people with alternative lifestyles and beliefs, which I found uninspiring, but had a much more uplifting day on 26th June at Spey Bay with Katie, my niece, and her boyfriend Chris. We had a lovely walk along the River Spey amongst the flooded woods, an area with interesting wildlife including dolphins and ospreys. We visited an ice house, part of a visitor exhibition and centre, and then had a cup of tea in their little flat which was within a set of houses owned by the Crown.

By now I had suffered two main setbacks. Seasickness had dogged my journey from the start to Northern Ireland. I was beginning to win that battle and now sailed without any seasickness tablets, which did me no good anyway because they seemed to depress me. I was able to sail in a moderate sea though I still did not venture out when a rough sea was forecast. This had led me to cut out the Scilly Isles and Lundy from my schedule. The engine failure had badly affected later stages and meant that Kippa and I had to pass by the beautiful Isle of Arran, which was very disappointing, as well as being a major factor in my deciding not to venture further north from Arisaig. At Findhorn I still had a slight boat leak and with the help of the boatyard eliminated the seawater intake from the possible causes. I finally resolved the problem by cleaning the rubber bellows carefully so that it seated to the collar. Kippa became perfectly dry inside from that time onwards.

However, now I had sorted out these issues there was an unforeseen problem that I could not overcome – the weather. I had expected some bad weather in Scotland but during three weeks of June it was miserably cold and wet. Even to mid-July it was very changeable and cold. It began to get me down in the Moray Firth and in some ways the toughest stage was coming up. Seasickness can be soul-destroying. Mechanical and boat leakage problems are frustrating but bad weather grinds you down and slows your progress and, because you can never change it, you feel powerless. A good night's sleep helps tremendously but getting rest aboard when the wind is howling and the rain pouring down is difficult.

To raise my morale, I spent the final Findhorn evening and a peaceful night with new friends Peter and Moira and this set me up for the next day. Peter had work to do but he delegated the farewell to Ian, who took some photos of Kippa as we left. Ian had been down to the boat the evening before to bring me a beer and his approach reminded me of an old friend, Harry Somerville, who had the same dry wit, gentleness and bright mind. I had met in Findhorn four of the kindest people on the trip, Peter, Moira, Ian and Elizabeth and they had all been very hospitable. I look forward to a return visit.

34. Findhorn to Whitehills

Boat festival

With tides moving from neap to spring, Wednesday 27th June was a safe moment to exit over the Findhorn bar. Ian came to see me off and I felt his encouragement and support. He was concerned that I should make it to Lossiemouth and later that day called me on the mobile phone to check up.

Indeed, it was not straightforward to get out of the harbour with a north-westerly headwind causing a swell that turned into turbulent breakers. The depth sounder dropped alarmingly at the stage where Kippa had previously grounded and registered only 2.6 metres at the bottom of one trough, so she was close to touching, even though it was 20 minutes before high tide.

There was swell out in the open beyond the fairway buoy so we headed out to deeper water. The wind was now creating a yawing broad reach which was uncomfortable, but I coped. The force was about five, so I had one reef in which took us along quickly. This was a sea of the type I experienced on the leg to Fowey the previous year. On that occasion I had been seasick the whole way; this time I was queasy but I was in control. I had learnt that it was essential to concentrate on steering, focusing on the land if possible and, if not, the horizon. The moment I started staring at a chartplotter, a compass or spent too long at charts below, I became unwell. At last I was able to sense the symptoms of trouble and work through them. If I felt myself going towards seasickness then I would work first to stabilise my stomach and then gradually over a period of an hour or two, recover. The autopilot had been banished to its locker long ago, only to be considered if we were to ever meet a millpond.

By Lossiemouth the wind had increased so I had taken in most of the jib and really needed to take another reef into the main, but with a strong swell I did not fancy having to deal with things on the foredeck so I made the best of it until I could get some shelter from the lee of land as we approached the port. The harbour entrance was very narrow and the sea was shaped like a sine wave between the piers. With the main not down fully and no ropes or fenders out, I drove Kippa into a tiny basin where there was sea still moving about. Without getting thrown onto the sea wall, I got the main down fully and then entered the east arm but found we were in a tight spot to get fenders and ropes on. I managed somehow and was glad to have someone catch the ropes when we came alongside the pontoon. Here I met Gavin and Sally who were also circumnavigating but in a rather classy Westerly Regatta 330 that was extremely well equipped. They were head and shoulders above me in terms of experience and confidence. They had only recently left from their East Coast base and were planning to complete the trip anti-clockwise and much faster.

Lossie, as it is known, is a town with shops dotted amongst the houses, so there is no real town centre, but there is a fine beach which you get to across a wooden bridge over the river. In all it is a fair place made better by an easygoing, cordial harbourmaster.

Next day we progressed to Portknockie, passing a fine view of the mouth of the River Spey, then past Buckie to the tiny harbour tucked inside a headland below a very quiet village that had clearly been devastated by the loss of fishing. The pub had the chummiest bunch of patrons I have ever come across; a rough mixture they were, but all good fun. While I watched Tim Henman on the big screen they encouraged me to cheer him on and showed no anti-English sentiment at all. Plenty of swearing and some banter but it was very good-natured. The pub served great whisky but no beer worth considering, as usual in Scotland.

Next day it was bucketing down with rain again, the wind was very strong and the swell considerable, so I caught a bus to Banff and then back to Portsoy to see the old fishing boats come in for the Scottish Traditional Boat Festival. Because of the weather, only one vessel made it from Buckie and that one, the Reaper from Anstruther, hit the pier wall. As the watching crowd gasped, I ran down and stuck a fender in between while the crew tried to fend off before a rope aft hauled them into the inner harbour and safety.

The Earl of Wessex turned up in his carbon-neutral Range Rover and country tartan kilt, before flying down south again. I imagine there must be a lot of trees in his name. Meanwhile, I ensured my own

113

carbon neutrality by purchasing an organically grown parsley plant. I had been concerned that somebody might hear me conversing with Scruff, the stuffed dog, so by cultivating a tiny garden I thought I might have a better excuse. Calling the plant Mr. Parslog may suggest I had gone mad but in fact the herb survived the rest of the journey, which shows that talking to plants may be effective.

To savour the splendour of Duff House I returned by bus to Banff. Duff House was built by William Adam, though its wings were never completed as planned owing to a dispute that sent Adam to an early grave. The building had some history as a hunting lodge on a grand scale but was left to rot after being an hotel and sanatorium last century. Fortunately some far-sighted people gathered public money and had the house restored without reference to cost. The result is tremendous. The ceiling of one room is exceptionally stylish and elegantly decorated, the wallpaper throughout is carefully selected, the furniture suitably in keeping and the chandeliers magnificent. Best of all are the paintings. There is an El Greco and two Gainsboroughs. There is one painting by Allan Ramsey, a Scottish artist, in a part Velazquez, part Goya style, that has a dress painted to equal those masters, even if there are a couple of faults elsewhere on the canvas that one could mention.

A grand piano, perfectly in tune, was available to play, so I did and of course that emptied the house of visitors. The staff were happy enough because it made it easier for them when the time to close arrived.

Next day Kippa and I continued from Portknockie to Whitehills, a short distance, thank goodness, as the swell remained unpleasant. I took the bus back to Portsoy again for the second day of the festival and found the port full of old boats that had now reached the harbour. There was quite a range, from coracles to paddle-driven steamboats as well as the lug-rigged Fifie.

Whitehills is the best marina for many miles, perhaps the best value in Britain at £15 a night. Showers work spasmodically, but there is a cheap laundarette and a room in which to relax in the dry where tea, coffee and biscuits are available, as well as a few books to read on those wet days (93% approx?). The harbourmaster is an exceptionally nice man who will introduce you to Jimmy, a local farmer, who picked me up and took me to his house to look in the freezer which was packed with fantastic beef. I bought some steak which was succulent and tasty.

35. Whitehills to Peterhead

Sun and fog

Keen to press on at any opportunity, Kippa and I set out from White-hills in horrid weather. It was dank and dismal. There was a thick mist of rain that soaked everything. I decided to abort the leg after just a couple of hours and turn into the industrial port of Macduff, a harbour down on its luck but still keeping going with ship repairs. The shops were sad but a café in a backstreet near the harbour was putting on a smart fresh face.

The next day was at last one to celebrate. There was great sailing and Kippa scooted along with one reef and a variable jib as the wind changed. I was able to optimise Kippa for speed and comfort and kept up between 4.2 and 4.8 knots to Gardenstown, which was bathed in sunshine, its houses soft pastel pink, purple and light grey, with many gable ends facing the sea. It is the kind of fishing village where they do not expect visitors because there are dangerous off-lying rocks; Kippa was twice as large as any other vessel in the tiny space behind the sea wall which served as the harbour.

I had arrived close to high tide to allow time to walk the path to Crovie, which was featured on David Dimbleby's programme where he discussed how it was unique in having houses that had gable ends at right angles to the wind. Perhaps artistic licence meant he overlooked Gardenstown, which has many similar cottages and is just around the bay.

In Inverness I had researched Crovie and found that no chart or almanac referred to it even though it had once been a fishing village. When I got to the pier I could see why: it was largely underwater, although there were the remnants of a structure, though unsuitable for a yacht to use. Along the seashore were remarkable red rocks. This was certainly a special place with a relaxed atmosphere but I needed to press on to Rosehearty while there might still be depth of water in the harbour. I had to miss out Pennan, the set for the film "Local Hero", because of lack of time but at Rosehearty the locals were again very friendly and spoke with an amazing accent which is fisherman's Doric. It sounds like a cross between Scandinavian and Geordie. The harbourmaster is a very friendly woman who was determined to welcome rare visitors and fight off the locals for me if necessary. There was no need, in fact I was presented with a couple of super mackerel by one fisherman.

It had been tight getting into this little harbour but next day it was even more tricky getting out. The wind was pushing in from the east and pinning Kippa to the quay. There was not enough space to spring off and there were mooring ropes and two dangerous sea walls to deal with. I could not do it on my own so I asked some locals, who were more than happy to help.

We rigged lines from the bow and people heaved from opposite piers. It was touch and go and only thanks to some good teamwork, people pulling at the right moment, that we avoided an expensive smash. Just as we came alongside the eastern pier end, I called for everyone to throw me the warps. They just managed to reach the foredeck in time for me to get the engine pushing Kippa forward and parallel with the quay. We could not head out into open water because there is a line of rocks alongside the entrance channel but once Kippa had gone a few hunderd metres north we could begin to head east to Peterhead.

Tuesday 3rd July the weather turned bad again and this was my first experience of really dense fog. The shoulder of Scotland north of Aberdeen is called Rattray Head. It is not as prominent as The Lizard or Portland Bill but it is very exposed to the North and East. Ideally one wants a westerly to turn the corner but I did not have that luxury.

I had been advised not to attempt this passage with any east in the wind. However, I did not want to be caught in Rosehearty with a northerly, unable to get out.

I was keen to sail and not motor in the fog so that I could hear other vessels but it was tough to maintain progress, with a water speed of only 2.5 knots and less than that along the route of my course because Kippa was having to tack. With such awkward conditions I had made sure to tell the coastguard our route. A Polish radio operator, who was on duty at the time, requested I provide my course and position. At one point she was very alarmed because Kippa's direction was towards rocks but she was reassured when I explained that Kippa did not beat against the wind that well and that we would be tacking off the coast very shortly.

The sea was slight and even smooth at one point but then a shape formed that I had not experienced before. It was as if a big heavy blanket was shuddering under the water. It was very eerie, listening for ships' motors, sailing slowly and being swished up and down in long shakes. I checked the chart and saw that there was a relatively shallow zone that we were crossing with variable depths. I headed out northeast to get into more consistent sea and, when it settled, turned southeast.

I considered diverting to Fraserburgh because of poor visibility but was concerned that we might meet a large prawn fishing trawler. I tried to get all the weather information I could and a helpful yacht relayed to me the wind further on. They were following a similar passage and were also in the fog. It was cold and miserable for hours but the connection with the other yacht and the coastguard kept my spirits up. I was encouraged even further when the other yacht called to say they had left the fog bank and the sun was shining. The wind was now coming in from the East South East but it was not of sufficient strength to kick up the sea and, about two hours later, Kippa came out of the fog. The world completely changed, the visibility was good and the coast was now sharply defined. I had been using the chartplotter and was wondering how long the batteries would last so I switched it off now that I could be sure of my position by sight. For the last hour I ran the engine to charge the batteries and motorsailed.

It was great fun entering Peterhead Harbour as they control movements of big oil supply ships. They were very courteous and seemed to tolerate all sorts from jet skis to tankers. Kippa was given the OK to enter as if she had been the Queen Mary. Indeed a supply ship was asked to wait for a moment while I crossed the harbour to the marina.

36. Peterhead to Arbroath
Kippa seeks her maker

The next leg was down to Stonehaven, then on to Johnshaven and Arbroath. Stonehaven was a pleasant spot, though the locals were a quite different breed from those on the Moray Firth, more connected with modern life and also rather aloof. Dunnottar Castle, perched on a sea cliff, was interesting and the wild flowers by the path were pretty, as were some of the gardens on the edge of town.

Johnshaven was an innocuous-looking entrance that turned out to be a devil. Clovelly has a tiny gap in the beach, Solva was frightening because of its craggy rocks, Cromarty could have been very tricky on a spring tide and Findhorn was a complete lottery, however, Johnshaven is a stealthy little beast. It looks harmless because the rocks lie just below the surface at the stage of tide you are likely to enter. The tidal stream at the entrance is not especially fast but it glides you subtly off line.

The leading lines are what make it very hazardous. There is a mark on a house which is nigh on impossible to identify for a visitor. In front is a yellow piece of plastic, about the size of an A3 sheet on a signpost. I positively identified it with binoculars only from about 200 metres. When I did, I judged my transit was not quite in line. Certainly the bearing you are given by the almanac helps but I had to ignore the ship's compass because the tidal stream was such that I was entering slightly crabwise to avoid rocks that can catch you from 200 metres out. In other words, there was not a metre for error.

In the end Johnshaven is just not worth the bother. The harbour is very prone to swell and causes uncomfortable conditions to stay aboard even in settled weather. Some locals are helpful but I was thrown off the quay (not literally) by a fisherman who seemed to think he owned the spot. The village is not unpleasant but there is nothing there to detain you for more than five minutes.

Thankfully the weather was calm and, after a moderately peaceful night, I took a bus to Montrose to find out about a distant relative, James Graham, 1st Marquess of Montrose. The view of him is mixed, depending on one's religious, political or moral perspective. He fought both against and for the King of England during the mid 17th century and was considered a brilliant military tactician.

The town of Montrose revealed another man of considerable achievement in a totally different field who has yet to be properly recognised. It might be too strong to say that he is another Michelangelo, but certainly his sculpture would stand up well beside Barbara Hepworth and Henry Moore. He lost part of his right arm in the First World War and had to learn to sculpt with his left hand. He then produced honest, painstakingly hewn statues and busts, mainly of ordinary people. Later in life he adapted his style and became more subtle, influenced by Moorish work perhaps.

Who is this sculptor? He is William Lamb. He had very little money and it was not until after his death that his statues were cast into bronze by the local authority who realised he was a genius. His study of a young boy is startlingly lifelike while the apparently simple little work called "The Whisper", of two women wrapped up against the weather, seems to float into another dimension. I know that sounds like art critic rubbish, but when I ventured to ask someone with a neutral standpoint, they completely agreed. "The Whisper" is not spooky but it is somehow other worldly.

Lamb's studio is now a museum, full of his magnificent work but also with two rooms left much as they were when he worked there. Admission is free and there is no commercialism inside, just a few cards and notelets. The curator is enthusiastic but realistic. There was none of the usual hype you get in museums.

It was amusing to think of the thousands queueing to see Michelangelo's David, cursing the Florence heat and then getting only a glimpse after hours of wait. There I was in a museum as the only visitor, able to talk to the curator and study the work of a great man in simple but perfect surroundings.

The trip south from Johnshaven to Arbroath featured some very fine red cliffs and plenty of seabirds. Kippa sniffed with her bow for local delicacies smoking from the houses of Auchmithie, the original source of the famous Smokie, until we reached Arbroath, a harbour of character where sympathetic improvement has been achieved.

From Arbroath I took a walk along the coast to investigate the fascinating cliffs with tiny beaches created between the high red rocks, made smooth by the whirling action of the sea. I also visited Dundee, which nowadays has a lot to offer and is no longer the poor relation of major Scottish cities. There is a fine contemporary arts centre and at Caird Hall I saw an outstanding guitar performance which was part of a small festival.

37. Arbroath to Edinburgh
Tea and cakes

Kippa and I then continued to Anstruther, one of a number of fine
fishing harbours including Cellardyke and Crail along the South Fife
Coast. Anstruther was rather noisy with its annoying funfair but
Cellardyke was a peaceful joy. Its harbour is secluded and the streets
are woven tightly with many houses to admire. Beyond the village playing field is a bracing walk along a rocky path to Crail, which is prettier
still. The inhabitants are quite upmarket so the gardens are well tended,
though it has not succumbed to over-gentrification. There was an
organic beauty about both the street pattern and the busy fishing
harbour that was very pleasing. Returning to Cellardyke by bus, I
happened upon the July church fête, a very spick and span affair
featuring tea served in the hall on dainty tablecloths bedecked with
flower arrangements.

At Anstruther I did some anti-fouling on the beach of the harbour
and then the next day Kippa and I tried to tackle a headwind to get to
Edinburgh. After four hours and progressing only a third of the way
with the sea cutting up more and more roughly I reviewed my plans.
Edinburgh was eight hours away at least, more perhaps if the wind
remained against us. North Berwick was not recommended by almanac
or locals. Kirkcaldy was a fair distance off and looked doubtful. Other
harbours on the South Coast of Fife were industrial and not geared up
for yacht visits. Calculating in my head, with Kippa tossing around too
much to start getting out the almanac, I decided to run to Elie. The tide
would be falling but I reckoned I could just make it. Tearing along with
the wind behind us, I became worried when I found I could not identify the harbour. The coastline undulated in a confusing way and the
settlements were hard to differentiate. I dithered and followed a wiggly
course trying to remain safe while still trying to make progress. Time

was running out when I finally saw a building known as the Granary. It was clear that it belonged to Elie. I kept sail up until close in, then switched on engine. We passed a buoy that marks a shallow and then dashed towards the pier end. I had to pull down sails at the last possible moment to avoid us being thrown onto the beach. We turned the corner of the pier as the wind howled in, to be confronted with a tiny corner that hardly constituted a harbour. There was a substantial sea-wall and then beach. On the beach small yachts and dinghies were moored. By the wall were a fishing boat, an old yacht and a rib. There was no room left, no mooring and insufficient space to raft up. I had to make some fast decisions.

I noticed a group of young lads who were jumping into the sea for fun. I called them over and asked them to get on board one of the boats by the wall. I managed to weave between the moorings, spin around and get Kippa towards a yacht. Somehow I got a rope over to one of the boys and asked him to tie it to the cleat of the other yacht. I struggled with fenders and then got another rope over from the stern. I clambered onto the other yacht and with the boys' help Kippa was saved.

They were a super bunch, up from Kirkcaldy, who sat politely in Kippa's cockpit, curious to know where she had appeared from.

The wind kept blowing all evening and in the end I decided to give in and find a bed and breakfast. Following the helpful advice from the pub, I found myself in a very plush home with a warm bathroom and comfortable bed.

From Elie I progressed to Edinburgh without any problem, sailing comfortably most of the way, amongst the oil tankers and other commercial shipping. I took up a mooring in the harbour at Granton, a rather uninspiring spot. I was now at the base I had planned for cruising with my daughters, however, when I went into the nicely furnished yacht clubhouse I discovered that a regatta was planned for the weekend and the place would be packed. The bar staff and the secretary did their best and did not try to get rid of me, which I thought very fair as they were bound to be chock-a-block.

As it turned out, the weather remained cold and miserable and when Monica and Rebecca arrived we took shelter in a backpacker's hostel. The new Scottish Parliament, the Castle, and the museum of the *camera obscura* became our ports of call. We spent one night aboard Kippa in Granton and when the weather improved a little we did manage two days of cruising in the Firth of Forth.

38. Edinburgh to Anstruther

Puffins

My daughter, Monica, now takes up the story.

"We were all worried about the weather because it had been awful the days before so the moment we saw a nice blue sky we decided to set off. We were taken by a kind man onto our boat, Kippa, which was on a mooring. Once we were there we put the suitcases in and everything was ready to go. We ended up leaving the harbour at about ten o'clock and we set off to the island of Inchcolm. The weather was lovely and the sea nice and calm. I don't remember much about the wind – I think it was quite good too. We arrived safely to Inchcolm where we visited an abbey, having bought a guidebook of the island as we had to pay something for landing. Half an hour later we were off to Anstruther. This second stage of the trip was a lot longer and the weather was not so good but we all enjoyed it."

What I remember from the trip is how cold it was despite the sun being out. Becky managed to stay warm enough to go onto the coachroof of Kippa but Monica got cold, even wearing lots of layers. In the end I got out my duvet from below and once she was wrapped in that she was comfy.

The sea was calm in the early stages of the trip but it did get choppy later. It was vital that the girls slept some of the way to guard against seasickness.

Becky recounts her story of the next day:

"We were in Anstruther Harbour moored on a pontoon next to a Hunter Horizon 272 that looked just like Kippa, but there was a difference – inside Kippa there were people sleeping on it: Daddy, Monica and I.

"We woke up on a sunny day with "Simpsons" clouds [the puffy cumulus ones], which wasn't really expected after a week of miserable weather. So, as we agreed the day before, we were going to go sailing to May Island. I was happy. I enjoyed sailing in good weather, I feel peaceful watching the sea and breathing the damp air. It is nice when you see you are on your own in the water and there are no cars or houses around you.

"Dad got the ropes ready, Monica helped him and I started the engine. We gently got out of the harbour and soon aimed for the north of the island. We got the sails up, turned off the engine and off we went. The journey was fine, the wind was just right.

"After a couple of hours we started to see lots of different kinds of birds. There was one that I particularly liked, it was the puffin; it has got a strange beak that makes it look beautiful and distinctive.

"Once we were next to May Island we had to find our way into the harbour. This was tricky considering there were rocks round the whole island. But then Daddy spotted the two white leading marks so we got them in transit and went through very close to the rocks but avoiding touching them. 'Aha' said Daddy when we at last found the tiny little mooring. It was a dangerous place so we only had a quick look round. We got off the boat and onto the slippery ramp, up a path and there it was, the wonderful scenery with thousands of birds standing on the rocks of the island with the stunning blue sea behind."

39. Anstruther to Eyemouth
Harbour seals

With the weather closing in again I did not want us to be miserable on the boat so I hired a car and we went up to the Highlands via St Andrews and Angus to Loch Rannoch. Then we toured down via Lanark and Haworth back to Surrey. After Monica and Becky had returned to Spain I took the train up to Kirkcaldy and two buses to reach Anstruther.

I was keen to move on to forget my sadness at the all-too-short holiday with my daughters. I always feel flat after my daughters have gone back to Spain. With them, life feels normal, without them it does not. My strategy to cope was to focus on the next leg.

Kippa and I crossed over to Dunbar in super sailing weather driving us along at an average of 4.5 knots. The wind was from the west and we could get across in one tack. Visibility was excellent and Bass Rock was sparkling with seabirds. I saw puffins, auks, gannets and all sorts that day.

Approach to Dunbar required some concentration and the advice I had received from further north was most useful. There are rocks below the surface to avoid and then the entrance is between a ruined castle and a large rock before you see the harbour wall.

Overconfidence brought me out the next day not realising quite how much the wind had increased. With only a piece of jib we were surfing at five knots. When I informed the coastguard of my passage plan they asked if I wanted the latest weather, a question never posed before which got me wondering. I welcomed all information available and they had force six at Fife Ness, which was strong but not too bad, so I pressed on a little further. However the wind grew stronger and, worse still, started to back. I could cope with a force six if it was on or behind the beam but I was not so sure I could cope if Kippa had to tack into it with the tide running with me to stir up the sea. The n se in he rigging had started to whistle a high pitched scream that I had never heard before.

I decided it was time to call it a day so I turned Kippa round and met the full fury of the wind during the turn. Nevertheless, I felt that Dunbar was the safer option than Eyemouth so we began to battle back into Dunbar. I considered raising some main to get more drive but found that the wind was building all the time so I decided to follow advice given by Dave, the former owner that in a strong wind Kippa does well with the jib tight in and the engine running. With a tide against me, I tried this approach and it worked. I was able to motor-tack. As we closed up to Dunbar, the main started to slip out of the straps that were holding it. I had no choice but to go on deck and sort it out. It was at this stage that I realised what a well designed boat the Hunter Horizon is. I was able to climb on the roof and yet feel safe. Kippa was being thrown around by the wind and waves but in the central point of the boat I was secure. This gave me enormous confidence in the capability of the boat. I had been up to the mast in bad weather but I had never before had to perch on the coachroof in conditions like this.

Once I had the mainsail under control it was a matter of getting into Dunbar without further mishap, which we managed.

Weather remained unsettled but two days later it was reasonable enough and Kippa and I had an excellent sail down to Eyemouth. During the voyage the wind switched round from northwest to southeast but its strength was just right for an enjoyable beat. The coast looked good and the birds kept me company.

Eyemouth is a good harbour, well protected, with a floating pontoon for yachts as well as full facilities as a thriving fishing port. The retired harbourmaster struck the right balance that ensures everyone mixes in. The showers are the best designed I have seen, modelled on the way they do it in Holland with shelf space for your clothes at the side so they do not get wet. Fancy marinas elsewhere in the country expect you to hang clothes on a couple of hooks, failing to appreciate that you have both the clothes you arrive in and the ones you are changing into, inevitably resulting in at least a sock in a puddle.

The weather worsened and I was pleased to be in a safe, comfortable spot. The town was not booming but the locals were making the best of what they had, attracting seals in to amuse the tourists, and offering some good fresh fish.

I met some very nice people in Eyemouth. Everyone along the pontoon was amiable. There was Laura next door, who had made an extremely admirable passage to Shetland. The crew of another boat had been at sea on the same day as I chickened out. They had also given up when they heard me on the radio. They related that they were reading force seven at the time.

Then there was Mousieu L'Hardi with a friendly family on board who later took some pictures of Kippa amongst the Farne Islands. Over the following days more were to come in while none left port. Some Germans arrived looking rather bedgraggled, then there were a Dutch couple who were most impressive. They had a fine boat that had no frills and a skipper of tremendous experience. Another Hunter came in, larger than Kippa, with a skipper who had made a passage from Peterhead in one go. No wonder that when he came alongside there was only one fender hanging on. I have rarely seen anyone more tired but we managed to get him alongside safely before he disappeard below, not to be seen again for 18 hours. As the weather got worse movement in the harbour stopped.

Now we were all waiting for it to stop touching force seven and settle into to force five if possible. The swell had been considerable at the harbour entrance and the rain lashed down causing quite a spate in the river. Lots of logs and brown water rushed into the harbour but at least it helped to hold back the swell coming over the rocks. The final entrant was a man from Edinburgh who arrived in a Snapdragon, a twin keel yacht that is difficult to manoeuvre. He was single-handed, had no lifejacket on, and looked, perhaps, 65 years old in his traditional sailing cap. He was beyond tired and his attempt to come alongside ended up with damage for Mousieu L'Hardi despite my best efforts. He reported that the wind had been fine coming out of Port Edgar but it had got steadily worse and Eyemouth was his only haven. I had been to my limit with seasickness but I had never been as tired as this sailor. It is frightening to see how one loses the capacity to think straight. To his credit, he remained calm and after a night's sleep was able to tell us more. Down below had become a terrible mess and he admitted he was not a long distance, heavy weather sailor; however, the fact that he had got into Eyemouth in an old boat in those conditions and with limited resources demonstrated he was no mug. I reflected that sea sailing sometimes takes you beyond your limitations and there is nothing you can do about it.

On the other hand, you are always learning new tricks. For example on one of the wet and windy days I took the bus to Berwick-upon-

Tweed to learn the art of sitting in a comfortable warm Café Nero for hours on end. The trick is to take a good book and not be afraid to spin out a sandwich, coffee and cake across several mealtimes. Better than getting cabin fever.

Gardenstown, Moray Firth (*above*), The Ouse, Lindisfarne (*below*)

Wells Harbour, Norfolk (*above*), Wells Quay (*below*)

A hungry seal in Eyemouth (*above*), Snape, Norfolk (*below*)

Felixstowe from Shotley marina

Seven Sisters, west of Beachy Head (*above*),
Golden Cap, Dorset (*below*)

Kippa dressed at Topsham. Dave Rolfe, former owner, is on the left.
I am on the right.

40. Eyemouth to Amble
Lindisfarne Ouse

At last the weather settled a little and so Kippa and I took a bumpy ride to Lindisfarne. I put on the autopilot to get some things sorted out and became queasy but quickly recognised the signs and immediately went back onto the tiller. The motion of the boat remained uncomfortable so I headed further out to sea and found it more reasonable. In time the stomach settled and I could enjoy the sailing. I was rewarded with a wonderful landfall. The island and castle can be seen when offshore from Berwick and this helped me navigate the coast. Round some ragged rocks we ran and then followed the transit of two vast pillars that mark the channel until the transit of a belfry and beacon lead up to a lagoon within an arc of beach that forms a natural harbour called The Ouse, a lovely spot for a twin keeler to anchor. Mousieu L'Hardi guided us into the ideal place to dry out.

When the sea receded I waded out to dry land, then explored the clifftop where you can enjoy a panorama of beach, wading birds and unspoilt coastline as far as the eye can see though I did detect a smell in the air which suggested industry was not that far off.

The village is lovely and Lindisfarne Castle stands impressively, even though it is not as architecturally pleasing as many of the Welsh castles. Best of all is the walk north along the island where the beach is deserted apart from sheep and birds. As you turn back inland there is a hide overlooking a patch of fresh water where you can view more of nature without disturbance.

On Friday 24th August I put up full sail and tacked off from the headland of empirical Bamburgh Castle to the Farne Islands. Mousieu L'Hardi, named after a French wind, followed us. We sailed into "The Kettle", an anchorage within Little Farne Island that is formed in the shape of an atoll. Part of land covers with water at high tide while the rest remains dry. On the western side is a gap into which you can sail at any state of tide. Kippa and I went in hoping to see seals, but without success so we pressed on.

A southeasterly persisted so we zigzagged down the coast until the wind died and we had to bob about until a stronger westerly blew off the land. It is a feature of this coast, so I was told by the locals, that the onshore wind created by a warm sun heating the land turns out to be a southeasterly, which is annoying if you are heading down the coast. The westerly was a much better proposition and Kippa began to catch up time lost earlier. I was very much in the mode of using only sail, which puts time pressure on the passage if you have a tidal harbour to enter.

I called up the harbour control to double-check my calculations and timings. As they were neap tides they reckoned I had time in hand and only at the lowest water might we have a problem entering Amble.

I tied up on the pontoon and quickly got a bag packed. I had a train to catch to Edinburgh where I planned to meet Sarah for the Festival. The marina owners were extremely helpful and gain second spot after Whitehills on my list of favourite marinas. I jumped in a taxi and then a train and discovered that Sarah was in the next train along the track.

We met up at Edinburgh station and had a great time, the highlights being "War On Worry" a comedy sketch show that was clean, funny and original, a Flanders and Swann remake, including the hippo song of course, and perhaps best of all, the Bavarian Symphony Orchestra who brought every phrase of the music to life. We had cheap tickets with the "gods" but in the second half we managed to move to better seats and really enjoyed ourselves.

41. Amble to Sunderland

Blyth Spirit

Having taken train and taxi from Edinburgh, we arrived late morning at Amble with time in hand to catch the tide and progress south.

Sarah and I set sail in the harbour, turned round the end of a pier and started to run down the main channel. It was a westerly but as we came down between the high wooden structures an eddy caused an accidental gybe. I had made a very incompetent start and startled Sarah although luckily no harm was done.

From then on, I ensured that the sailing went perfectly, setting two reefs and a small jib, which was sufficient in the force five to six, to send Kippa along merrily. Sarah was having great fun spotting the terns, kittiwakes, razorbills and guillemots and wanted us to head for Whitby. I had to explain that it was much too far and indeed, by the time we reached Blyth four hours later, she was tired enough and ready to step onto dry land. As she said, you cannot just stop and get out when you feel like it!

The yacht club at Blyth is an old lightship with a cosy saloon bar, peopled by typically friendly Northumbrians. The town itself is a long walk so we just did some beachcombing in the evening and again in the morning after a relaxed start to the day.

From Blyth, Sarah steered the boat very well, showing a natural ability with the elements, provided she was not distracted by a bird. The sea had settled and the offshore wind was force five so conditions were ideal for a terrific sail with one reef in to make Sunderland in good time. The outflow from the Tyne caused some unsettled water but the entertainment of ships coming in and out and seabirds on the cliffs kept life aboard very chirpy.

That evening, with Kippa tucked up in the marina, we took the Metro train to Newcastle for a Greek *meze*. The following day seemed favourable but when we checked with Hartlepool marina they reported 40-knot winds. Not wishing to risk such conditions we spent the whole day fretting because, on a tour of the coast by bus and foot, the wind never seemed that strong although we gathered that Hartlepool does have a microclimate where gusts can whip up in certain circumstances. South Shields was not exciting but a walk along the cliffs was more interesting. We came upon a hide and met a birdwatcher who talked us through the species we did not recognise.

By late afternoon we were very hungry so we tried a pub, thinking something simple would suffice. Unfortunately, Sarah was served with a reheated roast meal with an unidentifiable meat and I did my best to cut through some liver that had hardened like engine mountings from an old car.

42. Sunderland to Scarborough
Wave Wall

Sarah had to leave the next day to travel to Manchester where her daughter, Joanna, was playing with the National Children's Orchestra. Kippa and I progressed to Hartlepool with a wind of force five to six but again it was from a favourable direction. The marina turned out to be very large and rather soulless, while the town appeared even less attractive. A darkening sky threatened a storm but I had to meet Simon at the dilapidated railway station so braved the start of a downpour. Simon arrived as the heavens opened and we waited for a break in the rain. When there was a small let up after 20 minutes we splashed our way along the empty streets to Kippa and took shelter. We settled in and then the rain did stop, though the wind was strong. With no more time to lose if we were to reach Whitby, we headed out to sea.

At first we could sail on the jib with the wind behind us but when the wind dropped I had a dilemma. It was a dead run down the coast and the sea was still moderately rough. I knew this would create the problem that, with the mainsail up, Kippa would shake around and throw the boom across. I calculated that by beam reaching we would make no more than three knots on the rhumb line (the direct route) and that would make Whitby Marina inaccessible by the time we arrived because there is a swing bridge with limited opening times. It would also mean night sailing into a potentially dangerous and unknown harbour, even if we made do with a nasty sea-wall for the night. Reluctantly I put on the engine and we motor-sailed. It was not very pleasant but it was the wisest course of action.

Simon was typically phlegmatic and it was good to be together, enjoying a similar sense of humour that has remained with us since childhood. We made the best of the passage in the twilight and after about four hours we approached Whitby. You find the port set in a cleft of hillside and to enter you pass the navigation lights and work through a gap between two tall derelict lighthouses. In the dark they are a frightening spectacle, creating a sombre mood that put me in mind of momentous historic events, from sea battles to lost fishing boats. The ribbon of town still had an air of creaking inn signs, drunken sailors and press gangs despite the strings of lights that hung along some of the quay on the north side. Just in time for its last opening of the evening, we progressed through the swing bridge to a pontoon, where we were guided by another boat owner to a convenient space.

Facilities at Hartlepool had been basic but at Whitby they were a disgrace. Everyone knew it and yet somehow a solution had not been found and instead Yorkshire bloody-mindedness had created an impasse.

On Wednesday 4th of September the weather worsened and we decided to explore the ruined monastery and the town. The harbour had several interesting vessels and the view of the town from the hilltop was distinctive. It gave me time to reflect on progress so far. Yes, Kippa had come a long way, but the weather had been miserable since early June except for the odd day or two. If it worsened and autumn storms became the pattern then crossing the Wash was going to be a considerable challenge. In theory, I could go from Scarborough to Lowestoft but the distance was so great that a 24-hour passage was likely. I was not looking forward to the prospect.

The following morning we decided to venture out. We got through the swing bridge on its first opening of the day and found a trawler moving in the outer harbour. We thought it was going out to sea. It thought we were not. When we came to the lighthouses we could see why the trawler did not expect us to leave. We were met with a nasty sea as the north wind had kicked up some big waves overnight. We ploughed on and it got worse and within a couple of hundred metres the waves had reached a height of five metres and some were vertical. I considered turning Kippa round but with such a dangerous swell I feared we might be tossed against a sea-wall. I decided we would be best to continue out into the open sea. Simon looked very unsure how Kippa could get through these waves. I had every confidence in her. As a tall wave came onto us I angled her up any slope I could and managed to get her most of the way to the crest before the top of the wave piled onto the deck. Down the other side it was a matter of steering carefully to maintain control and seeking the best angle for the next wave.

Quite soon the wave height dropped down to a more manageable size and Kippa was able to get along without us being soaked. It was uncomfortable though and I hung onto the tiller. This time I was not going to pass over the helm and end up being seasick myself. Instead I concentrated on being positive, reassuring Simon by guiding Kippa over the waves and then turning her gently away from the wind as the sea shape improved. Simon was not enjoying himself but he made no complaint.

As we began to run down the coast southwards we were faced with the same problem as the day before, limited time and a following wind, so once again we had to motor-sail. I had worked hard to avoid using the motor since Inverness and had managed to sail most of the way but this was a second occasion to play safe. Scarborough was the only safe haven in the northerly we were experiencing and we had to get there before the water ran out of the tidal harbour.

I became slightly seasick but shrugged it off because I was in control of Kippa. I knew what had to be done to get us to Scarborough: keep a good course, maintain four knots and do my best to balance the motion of the boat so that we were reasonably comfortable. Being a tough soul, Simon does not normally feel the cold but this was another miserable 2007 "summer" day and I made sure he kept well wrapped up. Even he was surprised how bitter the wind was.

By the time we saw the castle on a high outcrop the clouds had broken a little and the sea was more tolerable. The northerly was not significant, though the swell remained, but once we were turning into Scarborough Harbour it became calm and we were able to come alongside a pontoon, with a hand from the harbourmaster and his assistant.

While Whitby had been a quirky town, Scarborough offered a more conventional seaside experience, some fine Georgian buildings on the hillside and, once past the tat of the strand, a couple of interesting shops. The yacht club provides economical, clean and tidy facilities which include a mini launderette and a decent sized shower.

We took tea in a French café and, to a background soundtrack of Mark Knopfler, I read the first words of famous books from their little library shelf while Simon guessed the title and author. Simon had fun proving his excellent literary credentials and too soon the time came for him to make his way to the station and return home. We hoped for a second chance for him to come aboard and do some proper sailing in Kippa.

43. Scarborough to Grimsby
Wrong side run down

The longest passage on my entire trip was 70 miles, from Scarborough to Grimsby. After using the motor from Hartlepool I was pleased to be sailing properly again. The sun came out and the temperature rose, the wind was pleasant and Kippa felt good as she slipped out of the bay. Progress gradually slowed as the sun beat down and by Flamborough Head we were moving very gently. The water became calm and I felt I could be at sea for ever in these benign conditions. Bridlington was the next port on the coast but I gave it a miss without a proper plan. A touch of madness brought on by the sunshine encouraged consideration of Wells-Next-The-Sea, which was a very long way off, but I thought perhaps I could anchor Kippa inside Spurn Head and continue south on the next tide.

Time slipped on; I anchored briefly south of Bridlington in idyllic conditions, the pale blue light sparkling through the ripples of the sea. After lunch and a rest I measured the distances and saw that it was many miles yet to the Humber Estuary. We continued south, now having to motor with the air becoming still.

By evening it was clear that getting inside Spurn Head would take many hours more so I called up John Cutting in Wales and had a chat to see what he thought about anchoring off Spurn Head; he knew the area from when he had lived in Norfolk. He gave sensible advice, including suggesting I call the coastguard, which I did. Having checked their charts, they came back saying that they saw no reason not to anchor where I planned on the seashore off Spurn Head.

Although the surface of the sea was smooth, the water was curling and swaying which caused Kippa to roll and bob. I was getting no rest so I was faced with trying to get inside Spurn Head to anchor, head for Grimsby or attempt Norfolk. I decided the latter was not sensible as I was already tired so I took Kippa into the Humber. Unfortunately the wind had returned from the west and the anchorage by the lighthouses looked uncomfortable so I had to face up to a night passage to Grimsby. I had not planned properly for this, though I had checked the basics about Grimsby and knew the tidal nature of the harbour. When we turned into the Humber it was littered with confusing lights. There were cardinals, red and green channel markers, pilot boats, ship navigation lights and shore lights. No wonder the lifeboat station at Spurn Head is manned full-time.

Working out which route to use was not simple. I plumped for the central channel as it looked shallower and I thought it might not have shipping. I was wrong.

All went well initially but, when we crossed the channel to be on the south side of the river to go into Grimsby, we met a ship coming out of the Humber. Being on the wrong side of the channel by normal regulations, we hugged the edge. As the ship closed up it twice did the five-hoot signal to ask for our intentions. I did my best to keep us out of the way but when we were alongside passing starboard to starboard a deck crew flashed a message at me which I could not decode fast enough but probably said, "You bloody fool". I was concerned we might meet another vessel so I called Humber VTS, who control shipping, and they asked me to go south of the next port-hand buoy which would take me out of the channel but still with sufficient depth for Kippa. I felt supported by the control officer and was not made to feel an idiot, even though perhaps I had been.

The final step had a further challenge because navigating into Grimsby fish dock at night is no joke. There are a mix of occulting (more light than dark) and isophase (equal light and dark) lights which are very difficult to differentiate. My brain can sense how long a flash is on but to sense how long it is off I find much harder. I wished I had equipped myself with a luminous watch with a stop watch facility to time the phasing and it was only with the guidance of the lock keeper that I could be sure of the route. The helpful officer talked me in on the radio by watching Kippa's lights telling me when to turn.

By now it was the middle of the night and I had been on the go for 18 hours. I found a pontoon and settled in for a good night's rest in the sheltered private marina, relieved to have survived a stressful and alarming landfall in the dark.

44. Grimsby to Wells
Soft Wash

It was a peaceful night and I gently eased myself up in the morning to talk to the very pleasant harbourmaster, who was an experienced yachtsman. He asked how long I was staying and I told him I planned to leave in the afternoon. I was making the most of the high pressure and I was determined to get across the Wash, one of my last major hurdles, during good weather. "Oh no, you won't," he replied "There is a dredger coming in." I was surprised that a dredger would be that much in our way so I asked him if he was certain. He made some calls and found that there might be a few minutes after the dredger finished when we could slip out of the dock, but I would need to listen to the port radio and keep abreast of developments. He insisted that if the dredger was working there was no chance of getting out.

The marina is owned and run by the berth holders who must be top-notch sailors by the look of the large sturdy boats on the pontoons; these were yachts prepared for crossing the North Sea in gales. The kinds of boats you meet in a port give a clear indication of the distance people have to sail from the harbour to go cruising and the kinds of conditions they encounter on the way. On the South Coast you get a lot of modern boats that are built as much for cabin comfort as for sailing; for example, in Chichester there are large posh yachts that never go beyond East Head, where there is an anchorage within the harbour. In the drying harbours like Penzance and Solva, yachts are quite small but they are very workmanlike. On the East Coast you are more likely to see traditional tough designs because even the hop to the next harbour is a challenge. Crossing the English Channel is a considerable undertaking, but crossing the North Sea from the Humber to Holland must be quite another matter.

I tidied up and made careful plans for the next stage of the journey, having been slapdash the day before. I listened to the radio and at 1 o'clock I looked out of the hatchway and saw why I shouldn't to argue with the dredger. Instead of the usual flat-bottomed craft with a scoop it was a ship that towered over the buildings. I marvelled at the skill of the captain at getting such a large vessel into the fish dock. What he had done was edge through the lock and then slide along the quay to get the vessel's nose into the entrance of the marina. Just the bow took up the space of a trawler. On the foredeck was a large machine with a big double bucket which was hoisted over the side with great skill and dropped into the water to pull up the silt. The way the operator swung the bucket round and over the hold to drop the load was very slick and completely under control.

The radio traffic was virtually constant and other boats were queueing to get in or out, knowing that the tide would mean the dock gates would have to be closed at about 3 o'clock. At 2.30 the ship eased back a little and we were allowed to slip out from the marina and out of the fish dock.

Kippa and I made our way down the Humber to the anchorage inside Spurn Head, which is behind the pier where the lifeboat and pilots launch. I was hoping to go one better than anchoring if conditions were right and I had very carefully calculated a time to beach in order to have a walk on this famous spit of land. All went well and we came into a precise depth, the wind was light and the beach seemed clean. We gently grounded and a lifeboatman came out of his house and had a good look but saw that I was not concerned so went back in again. When the tide had fallen I tried to climb out but found that the drop from the stern was more than usual and I could not quite make it to the ground and be sure to be able to climb back in later. I considered trying to rig a ladder but decided instead just to enjoy the peace, the sunset, the view of the disused lighthouses and the serene panorama of our little bay.

I had supper and then rested. I knew I would not sleep but I also knew that resting is nearly as good and sure enough I got a couple of microsleeps through mind over matter. At 9 pm I got a decent sleep until 10.20 and then again until 11.30. When my mind started buzzing I got up and made ready for floating off.

Engine trouble in the Firth of Clyde did not faze me, grounding at Findhorn had been a nasty moment but we had coped, staying calm for my crew when we met steep waves out of Whitby took some resolve and Grimsby at night had been very daunting. But now I was to get the fright of my life that put everything else into perspective.

Kippa floated off the beach just after midnight. I had become disorientated by the pilot book diagram and local advice so I had to make sure to identify positively every single light through binoculars. As soon as we were set up I checked the traffic movements with Humber VTS, letting them know that I was planning to go across the shipping channels from the north to the south side of the Humber Estuary. They asked me to wait for three ships and I watched as I saw their navigation lights go by. Then they gave us the all-clear. I moved Kippa out to the pilot jetty, taking great care to maintain a clear picture of the arrangement of lights. I found we needed to swing left more than I imagined, but I was certain of our position and bearing. We moved out from behind the screen of the pilot jetty and I looked up the estuary to see if any ship was on its way out. Lots of red and green lights, but all flashing. Nothing fixed. We entered the main channel and I looked out to sea. Oh my God! My heart missed a beat. There was a fixed red and green light and a white light between and above. Worse still, the lights were quite a distance apart and high up. As this went through my head, my jaw probably dropped. A large ship, the Auto Progress she was called, was coming straight at us and it was mighty close. I heard Humber VTS warn the ship about me, then called them to check I was doing the right thing, asking if I should turn round and get back out of the channel. They were much calmer than I was and told me to press on, which I did, holding my breath. I was partially relieved when the starboard light disappeared and I could see only the port light, however, I knew we were not safe because I reckoned on the ship having to turn towards us, since there was a bend in the channel at this point. All Kippa and I could do was press on across the channel at right angles to get out of the way as fast as possible.

I have to admit that I did not have the courage to look round so I never saw that ship again. I did not dare to turn and see her from the side. In theory, I should have turned onto a parallel course if it was going to hit us so that the impact would have been lessened but I just felt it best to hold my nerve and keep going. I doubt I would ever again have night sailed if I had seen that monster as close up as it must have been. I just kept on course. I did not exactly wait for the bang, I just told myself that there was nothing I could do about it except concentrate on steering straight. I looked for the next buoy on my list and steered for it.

Once across the estuary I set our course southeast. I listened to the bridge-to-bridge radio conversations and was amused to hear a German ship telling off a Russian ship for not being clear about its navigational intentions. The Russians shrugged off the criticism and I could sense the German fury. There was no wind so I motored with the autopilot and kept awake with coffee and watched the big tankers from afar going into the estuary in line, like aeroplanes landing at Heathrow. Obviously my slot in the scheme of things was a short one and the gap that Humber VTS had given me was as good as they could offer. The speed at which those ships go, means that you have a very short time to cross.

Once into the shallower waters of the North Sea, where large ships cannot go, I began to calm down. I ticked off from a complete list of the buoys we would pass on the way to Wells-Next-The-Sea. I focused on my night navigation, seeking the next light on the list, a flashing red. When I found it, I watched intently for its rate of flash. Two short flashes. No, three. Wait. Long and short. Hang on, two buoys with different sequences. I checked the chart. No, only one buoy. I looked again with binoculars. I watched and studied, timed and counted. Not two, three buoys, roughly in a line. I looked again at the chart. Only one red buoy. Perhaps the others are not marked, I thought. Maybe they are new. Try the chartplotter. No better. Look again. Definitely three distinct locations but the phasing is impossible to measure.

This went on for half an hour. I looked for other buoys but none was visible. By my reckoning I was still a way off from the next buoy and the GPS confirmed it. So what was going on? I decided to stop letting it worry me. I looked around elsewhere, trying to make out other objects or at least the loom of a town. A strange black box appeared. What could that be? A ship? No, too square. A building? No, still too far off-shore. An illusion? Yes. A reversed mirage. It is an effect I have noticed before, where the brain is unable to decipher the eye's input so it just blacks it out.

I had a little chuckle at myself and relaxed, ignoring the flashing light and continuing on the bearing I was confident was correct. A while later, when I looked again, the red light had a phase that made sense and correlated with the chart. But where were the other two lights? Gone. Because it was one light all the time, it was just bobbing under the horizon and when it reappeared the change in the position of Kippa's deck meant that it appeared to be a different light. As we came past that red light I smiled. It had given me the runaround but looked completely innocent now.

An hour or so before dawn, a pink moon briefly showed an enigmatic cusp with a tiny triangular snub nose that might have been the Man in the Moon. A final thin arc faded away and the coming sunrise began to burn the horizon a rich orange which became steadily more intense. I discovered that if I stared at the orange stripe and then switched my focus to the sea or high in the sky, then the colour became even more vivid. By casting my eye across the scene, I found that the orange appeared paler.

Kippa and I were north east of the Wash as the blue light of day began to fill the sky. The shore lights had disappeared and sea was all around, with no indication of land in any direction. It was some time before a radio mast planted in the sea showed as a distinctive and encouraging beacon.

After several more hours and a staggered breakfast, I could see the thin edge of Norfolk. The tide had been variable, sometimes with us, sometimes against and sometimes across, but overall it was roughly as expected. We had made very good time – indeed, it was much too early to enter Wells, so we now had to wait for the tide. By means of dawdling and anchoring, time was used up. I considered going for Blakeney and made several phone calls to get local advice. People were very helpful, especially Charlie Ward who runs Juno, a traditional boat that sails out of Morston Quay near Blakeney. With the neap tide he advised against entering Blakeney so I talked to the harbourmaster at Wells to find out the earliest time to come in. He said he would meet us at the fairway buoy about 3 pm and indeed he did, leading us in with the harbourmaster's launch. I felt relief and joy as we approached the wonderful river. We threaded our way through the sandbanks along a tight little channel that I began to realise was the finest landfall of the lot. No mountains, no quaint houses and no grand castle. Instead, it was a golden strand of beach, then marshland and then boats of all sizes playing, working or lying lazily. Wells-Next-The-Sea. Gorgeous. A simple little paradise.

We were put on the pontoon next to a Southerly 110 lift keel yacht. A smart vessel, with attractive lines that suggested practicality below and seaworthiness on the move, her skipper was David Hadlow and her ship's dog was Holly. David was also a circumnavigator but he had already finished and was back in what was his home port. He was a kindred spirit, not a dyed-in-the-wool seaman nor a type with outrageous stories to tell; I admired his unassuming and modest nature. He oozed common sense and a rational respect for the sea gained from visiting many awkward harbours. We got chatting over tea and later, at his birthday party shared with other sailors, I discovered he had sailed his little ship into Burnham, which has no marker buoys, by means of recording GPS positions during a reconnoitre at low tide to establish the channel layout.

The setting of Wells quayside gladdened the eye. It was convenient too, next to the excellent facilities with nobody to bother us and so much to see. The tide falling and rising changed the landscape constantly, the birds entertained and if a visitor had a need to wander, the town offered a varied selection of shops, despite being only two streets' worth. The grand square at the end of the main street was a thick grass expanse dotted with fine trees and surrounded by elegant buildings, the highlights being two inns.

In the sunshine I sat down to enjoy the scene and contemplated that Kippa had crossed the North Sea from Yorkshire to East Anglia. From Scarborough to Great Yarmouth is a trek but we had broken the back of the journey and I could now unwind a little. I bought some drawing equipment in the friendly artshop and did a sketch of a tree, applying a new technique for me, brimming with confidence and personally at ease. I could have stayed in Wells for a week and seriously considered doing so. Why go any further when this part of the world felt so special?

45. Wells to Aldeburgh

As long as we don't get a southerly

It was with a heavy heart that I decided to leave Wells. I had gathered information on the weather patterns and a new system was due to break up the high pressure. I had to recognise that Great Yarmouth was still 50 miles away and there were no havens of any kind in between.

Foolishly, I failed to take in the relevance of some local information. Apparently a pure westerly is very rare in these parts. A south-westerly or north-westerly is common enough and the ideal scenario is to leave with a depression passing the West Coast of the British Isles. I had incorrectly associated the high pressure with good weather.

One of the factors that was weighing in favour of my leaving on Sunday 9th September was the time of tide and daylight hours. High tide at Wells would be first thing in the morning, meaning that 12 hours later I would have the tide to carry me up the River Yare to Great Yarmouth. Hence, daytime sailing. While I generally enjoy night sailing, it can be hairy and after the Humber I reckoned I could do with maintaining sanity.

A further piece of local advice that I did not fully take on board was that Lowestoft is a better choice than Great Yarmouth.

When I looked out of the hatch at sunrise there was hardly a breath of wind. I set off after breakfast and made my first error. Although I had had plenty of time to study the channel, I had failed to take a note of the first 300 metres from the pontoon so Kippa grounded on the very first sandbank. Fortunately she had been moving gingerly, aware of my lack of foresight. As I had taken the precaution of leaving on a rising tide, she came straight off the bank and was able to continue. Now I took great care, following the marks religiously, remembering as best I could the course taken with the harbourmaster. I also used the chartplotter, which I had left on during the entrance so that I would have my course traced on leaving.

As we came up the channel, the tide tried to push us back in but by the time we were out of the lee of the woods it had gone slack. Once we were out beyond the fairway buoy heading out to sea, a northerly was picking up. I called the coastguard for the latest forecast. Not too strong, but north; there was a suggestion of a westerly later, though probably too much later. I actually considered turning round because I was so sorry to leave behind Wells when there was so much to explore along that coast but I would be re-entering on a falling tide and feared being grounded by the swell. No, we were committed, so on we went with full sail up, though I was not feeling great. Blakeney Point passed on the starboard side and the sea conditions improved a little as we managed to get offshore. I was hoping the wind would stay north and enable Kippa to turn onto a nice beam reach and then a broad reach, but it just did not seem to happen. As we curved round Norfolk the wind seemed to laugh at us, veering gently round. It was hard work to keep up any pace when the tide turned against us, and when the wind died we were obliged to motorsail, in order not to be feathered onto what was a lee shore. There were some commercial ships to keep me company, the most interesting being a coaster which I called up to check their course so as not to impede their progress. Some minutes later a highly professional Irish voice answered, confirmed the ship's course and we swapped a greeting of encouragement.

When the tide turned again six hours later we were at Sea Palling and were able to sail without the motor and make reasonable progress. At last it was a beam reach; I just wished the wind had been stronger. The sun was out and things went well for an hour or two until the placid airs seemed to fade gently. I expected it to return from another direction but more strongly. I was hoping westerly or at least south-westerly. No such luck. When it came through it was distinctly brisk and right on the nose, fully south, so now we really had our work cut out. We were in the shallow trench between the Middle Scroby sandbank and the coast. The tide was now ripping us along at three knots but the wind speed was definitely force five against us. With a shallow variable sea bottom the water churned up dreadfully, turning yellow with sand. It was concerning because it felt as if we were close to the sea bottom even though the chart said it was safe water. I knew this to be a troublespot where sandbanks shift. I was also coming to the conclusion that Lowestoft was too far and I needed to get into Great Yarmouth somehow.

An added worry was that the area was becoming like a building site. Two oddly shaped vessels were at anchor in funny places and even when we were able to avoid these I could see a muddle at the river entrance. The harbour controller was very laid-back and gave me guidance, explaining that there were extra buoys marking the construction work. There were also vessels on the move here, as well as activity within the harbour, so we had to wait our turn. We got into the river all right and then carried the tide upstream. At least we had made it in time for the rising tide; the River Yare was running exceedingly fast and it would not have been a sensible idea to fight the ebb.

At the town quay the river was thrashing along as I turned into the current and came alongside. It was a devil of a job to get onto a ladder and tie up with bollards perched high up on the sea-wall. Rigging a fender board was very awkward too and I was not happy with the arrangement I concocted. On arriving at port I might normally settle and take time to rest, but not on this occasion. I had supper and a brief stroll ashore, then turned in for the night – but it was not long before I woke up.

I thought I was dreaming at first. Apparently Kippa had gone off for a sail on her own. Had she finally gained a personality and was homesick? The water was rushing past the boat, on both sides. We were not next to a quay. I jumped up and looked out of the hatch and to my horror we were out in the river. Poor Kippa was clinging on for dear life and the river was now ebbing out like crazy. The whole of the Norfolk Broads, including the massive Breydon Water, were on their way out to sea. Kippa, who was warped quite normally with spring lines, had been pulled out into the stream and told by the river to join in with the fun. The cackling water flew past, taunting poor Kippa while I wondered what to do. I pulled on some clothes and then pulled on some warps but it was useless. The stream was getting stronger and it was not just speed, it was somehow the weight of water. The ropes were at full stretch and I was worried the cleats might give up. Time to call for help. There was nobody about at midnight on what had become a cold night so I radioed the harbour control. They were helpful and put a pilot boat onto the case immediately. It was not long before we had company and from the shore Kippa was being hauled in. She came alongside as grace-fully as she could and at last the water was rushing past only one side. All available ropes were put to work and we took quite a time adjusting her this way and that before she would settle parallel to the quay. I did go back to bed for what it was worth, though respite was not likely. But

I did sleep because I remember dreaming all sorts of catastrophes including white water-rafting the Iguazu Falls (a vast area of cataracts between Argentina and Brazil).

Great Yarmouth has some interesting tidal characteristics. Slack water, when the river is flowing neither up nor down, occurs about an hour and a half after low water and high water. This means that the water at the town quay is rising while the river is flowing downstream. After high water, when the level is highest up the wall of the quay, water continues to flow upstream. The way I explain this to myself is to think of the sea as a plug. The sea blocks the water at low tide and so the stream flowing out from the Broads fills up the river like a bath. When the tide turns at sea, the plug comes out and the river can then let the water run out of the bath.

A pointer I was given by the locals was that the flow of water on the surface can be different from the flow deeper down in the river. In addition to this, there are eddies such as the one caused by the bridge above the town quay. What it all adds up to is that you should give Great Yarmouth a miss if you possibly can and head for Lowestoft. It is only a few miles away and the harbour is by the sea, not miles up-river. Having said that, I think there may be a way to tie up temporarily near the mouth of the Yare at a boatyard that has diesel. It is a wooden and rickety quay but it is much closer to the sea than the town quay. Alternatively, you can cross Breydon Water to where the tide is a bit weaker, provided the bridge will open for you.

In the evening of Tuesday 11th September I let go of the quay and drifted down the river, crabwise, with the tide. A large supply vessel radioed to ask our intentions. I replied that we could speed up or drop back as he wished and his reply was more or less "I don't mind what you do as long as you realise that once I start going I cannot stop". I replied that I would pull up by the quay and let him by. Voyager filled about a third of the width of the river, dwarfing Kippa as she passed.

We tagged along behind at a safe distance and then followed out to sea. We did our best to sail but there was not a breath of wind so we had to motor, though it was not for long because the spring tide was ripping along the coast at over two knots.

Lowestoft is a simple harbour and marina and the safest haven for many a mile. You have to go a very long way to match it for ease and convenience. The clubhouse is very plush and right beside the pontoons. It felt a little bit too commercial, though it certainly has a comfortable bar.

Continuing down the coast, we had to do some more motoring but then the wind improved and we were able to sail, if in a rather leisurely manner, to the River Ore. The Orford Bar is notorious because it shifts regularly. I had been over it before but I still gathered up-to-date information and had a detailed entrance chart with all the critical depths marked. The pilot book was also useful and it was not a problem to follow the rules, such as staying close to the buoys, then keeping right along the beach before placing ourselves in mid-channel.

The wind was picking up nicely as Kippa crossed the shallowest point and we were sucked up the river by the strong tide to Orford, where we stopped so that I could pump up the dinghy. The man in charge of the quay was distinctly unwelcoming and for the first time in Britain, he did not offer to take ropes as we came alongside even though he clearly had nothing better to do. He made it very plain that we were not welcome and should shove off at the earliest moment. Fortunately another man who had been a mariner was more kindly and despite his advanced years offered help. I did not trouble him but I stopped to chat so he could reminisce. An onshore easterly was now blowing well and Kippa sailed up the river at great speed, with Rolly tugging behind. The Ore is a stunning sailing river, gently winding between the spit and the land until it reaches Aldeburgh. I took up a mooring just beyond the village and rowed to shore to explore it.

Aldeburgh has been discovered. Once a backwater, it is now on the map and exploiting its status. The boatyard has failed to keep up with the times and was in a mess. When I went into the chandlery I was attacked by the dog on guard, so Aldeburgh is a place I shall not bother with again – which is a pity, because there are some lovely buildings and gardens.

46. Aldeburgh to Snape and back
Running aground

I had recently missed out on Blakeney in Norfolk but now I had the chance to get to Snape, on my shortlist of places to which I particularly wanted to take a sailing boat. I had previously attempted the trip with four friends in a chartered yacht but we got little further than Aldeburgh before grounding. This time I wanted to see if Kippa could do better. It was a day after the best of the springs, which lent a particular frisson for if we got stuck fast, we would be stranded for two weeks until the spring tides returned.

The weather was fine and the wind was good. My strategy was to go up at half tide so that I could see the channel while the mudflats were visible. From the mooring by Aldeburgh the channel is wide but it gradually narrows and twists as the hamlet of Iken comes into view. I had the chartplotter on and a good paper chart prepared but I knew that I could rely on neither.

Kippa and I took it gently so that if we grounded we would float off. The channel marks consisted of withies, small branches, sometimes marked with something red or green. I looked to see if there was some other distinguishing feature but I could not see one. We got as far as Iken, sailing gently along, and then suddenly stopped. It was odd because we were right in the middle of the channel as far as the withies were concerned. It was still three hours before high tide so there was no panic but to have grounded in the channel and at half tide was a mystery. I looked around and saw a traditional small boat being steered in our direction. They sailed up to Kippa and I told the helpful couple we were stuck. They were equally surprised that Kippa was not floating, considering we had not come out of the channel.

Fortunately I was soon able to get moving again by reversing, using the motor. We followed the other boat but got stuck by deviating a little out of channel. With a lifting centre plate they were able to get moving though they later got stuck again and had to use their outboard motor. Kippa and I gingerly continued trying to see where they went in the channel but also looking for clues to the course of the river. We passed the pretty Iken church and a small piece of higher ground referred to as cliffs on the chart but which were only perhaps ten feet high and made of earth. We progressed a little further and got stuck two or three times while the small yacht continued on. I got out the leadline and took measurements to ascertain where the deeper water might be. With considerable difficulty we got off again. A little further on I was faced with a stretch of water that looked simple enough but was a trap. It was a large shallow flooded lagoon and the channel was not through it but round it. In the distance I could see a small stick and so we aimed for that and found the route. Yet more stops and goes, twisting and turning in a channel that was only the width of the length of Kippa until finally I could see Snape in the distance. It was now about one and half hours before high tide. There was a path by the river and we could almost step off. I could have called to the walkers as we grounded again in what appeared to be the centre of the channel. I looked around. There was no clue to suggest which way to go. There were no more withies ahead. The leadline offered no definite data. The chart was ambiguous. I backed Kippa off by motor and considered. Would we get permanently stuck if we continued? I almost decided to pack it in and return downstream but I thought, no, this time I am going to go for it and to hell with the consequences. I chose a route in the middle of the channel and slowly motored forward in hope and we just managed to make it to the quay. I jumped off and had a quick walk around. The café was very inviting and I chose a cream tea, with coffee not tea. It was scrumptious. Lovely scones, good jam and lots of cream and the real ground coffee was reviving. I could not dally so I took a couple of photos and jumped back onto Kippa and set off. I asked a local where the channel might be in the Snape approaches and he suggested the south side offered the best depth. If so, we had been lucky to get away with coming up the middle of the channel.

There was still half an hour before high tide but, knowing the depths I had encountered and the fact that downstream of Snape the tide would be turning any moment, I had to come up with a better strategy. Then I remembered a technique I had used on the charter boat in the Deben at night, close to Woodbridge: surveying as you go. Fortunately the electronic depth sounder was working reasonably well and by supplementing with the leadline I determined I would be able to judge the shape of the river bottom.

At the first corner, instead of just following what I believed to be the channel, I eased Kippa towards the side of the river and watched the depth. If the depth sounder was working correctly the reading would go down from say 1.7 metres, to 1.5, then lower as we came out of the centre of the channel. When we turned back into the channel the number would rise. If the number flashed, that indicated the electronic sounder either could not obtain a proper reading or we were about to ground. So with this method we zigzagged down the channel. It seemed to work. It was impossible to remember the route we had come, but with this method progress was trouble-free, if very nerve-racking. I dared not lose concentration for a moment.

About half an hour after we left Snape the tide had turned and the water level was dropping. If we grounded now it would spell disaster. With time running on and tide running out, we had to make swift progress so I pressed Kippa on a little more quickly. We nearly came unstuck, stuck I mean, when the depth sounder flashed. I turned Kippa back into the channel just in time. We were going too fast; I could not assess the depth at the speed we were going. I throttled back and continued on with care and as much speed as I dared. We came upon another yacht at anchor. I stopped to ask advice and he said that the withies with a bushy top were starboard marks. However, he also said that some of them had lost their bushy tops so one could never be sure. Well, I suppose it was of some help; at least it meant that if I saw a bushy top that would be starboard. If it did not have a bushy top it could be either.

The withies were also very variable in their distance apart, random in fact, and often I could not be sure which way to turn. On certain curves that took us along the shore, there would be some sense to their position but where the curve ended and a straight or a reverse curve started, it was a confusion. The "survey method" seemed the best option so I continued with that.

At Iken a fairly large traditional gaffer was running up-river. He was sailing with such confidence it was very disheartening. How could he come up at this state of tide to Snape? I felt a little better when he stopped and picked up a mooring buoy. Kippa and I slipped past and I decided to regain some pride and sail, no matter what, and this we managed. It was tricky though, tacking in what was still a tight channel, but I was determined to have the pleasure of sailing on this beautiful day in this tiny creek.

In time, we passed Iken church and were out into wider, deeper water and could sail confidently on. I took up the mooring where we had been before, to have a short break before continuing down-river. I thought to myself "Pride comes before a fall" but felt so happy to have reached Snape that I celebrated anyway, with a cup of tea.

After my rest I was ready to set off again. The wind was blowing nicely so I decided to sail off the mooring. I raised the main and let go the rope – at the wrong moment. Kippa started sailing towards the bank. I tried to tack her but she was moving too slowly so I had to fall back onto the tack towards the bank. By now we had slipped down with the tide and on a second attempt to tack we grounded, so that was that. The tide was going out fast so there was no way we would get off. It was a very basic and silly set of errors.

As the tide went out Kippa slid to a leaning angle and then sank into the mud. I calculated the tide and it was going to be in the middle of the night when we floated again. I assessed the situation and decided to row out in Rolly, the dinghy, with a rope to the mooring, however, I discovered that the tide was too strong and the rope in the water pulled with the tide. I considered putting on a second rope to add length but decided instead to wait for the tide to slacken. I had some supper and then, with just enough water to get into the dinghy and with the tidal flow very slow, I managed to get the rope onto the mooring. Now I had to wait. My concern had been that the wind might increase and push Kippa further onto the mud when the tide returned.

The stars came out and it was a beautiful evening. I had a short sleep and then looked out again and all was still. A depression that was coming over from the Atlantic had not arrived.

At one o'clock in the morning Kippa began to move. I got on deck and made ready with the mooring rope. I felt Kippa rise upright and pulled hard on the warp but we did not budge. I waited, listening to the birds calling. I was worried that if I did not manage to pull in fast enough on the rope, Kippa might swing round on the in-coming tide and hit another boat on the next mooring. A short while later Kippa floated free and I pulled as hard as I could. We glided across the water with perfect ease, flying like an arrow which made it easy to carry the mooring rope along the deck and hitch Kippa by the bow. I cleaned up as best I could and settled down, though it took a while for the adrenalin to dissipate. I was relieved to be off the dangerous shore and could finally appreciate the sounds of the birds as I fell asleep.

47. Aldeburgh to Butley

Lost ashore

Some parts of the journey were fun, some boring and some shear endurance. From Aldeburgh to Butley was a good trip but ended in an unexpected turn of events.

With a steady wind from the south, Kippa and I had to tack down the Alde. Tacking down a river with the tide carrying you along is one of my favourite sailing experiences whereas tacking from harbour to harbour with a limited passage time can be a pain due to tidal gates, such as needing to pass a headland before the tide turns. In river sailing I enjoy the battle with the elements, trying to get the best from the wind and the boat, maximising tide down the middle of the channel, working to tack fast and smooth to maintain speed. Down the Alde I was also working to pick my moments to angle each tack round the bends to minimise the number of tacks while still optimising all the other aspects. This meant going right to the edge of the channel, working to read the shape of the mudbanks, following the chart but not relying on its accuracy, aware that the banks shift.

It was pleasing to have full sails up, Kippa leaning over, lots of speed, quickly taking us down past the Cold War listening station with its radio masts and concrete buildings, to one of the prettiest little ports on the East Coast, Orford.

I took up a mooring and rowed across to the quay. Here again was the quay master wanting to turn me away if he could find an excuse. He could not and reluctantly let me come ashore to shop in the village. I walked up the street, lined with ornamental fruit trees on carefully mown verges, backed by colourful old cottages that put me in mind of a Miss Marple whodunnit film set. Beyond the village square was a mound topped by a large keep, set in grassland which had been allowed to run to a mix of wild plants. Without encountering the over zealous approach that can occasionally tarnish National Trust properties, the public could go up close without paying and lie on the grass to drink in the atmosphere undisturbed. The post office-cum-village shop was poorly stocked and managed by one unfriendly and one friendly assistant. Down the road was a church where two ladies were clearing what may have been harvest festival. Everywhere in Orford signs abounded suggesting that conformity was king. Back at the quay, I bent down to untie Rolly and cut my hand on the poorly maintained rusting steps. Once aboard Kippa, I was careful to apply disinfectant to ensure no long-lasting effects. Beautiful though Orford was, I was happy to move on.

I sailed on down to a little island in the river seeking an anchorage and then chose to turn up the Butley River where I came upon a tranquil backwater that became so lovely that it reminded me of Dedham Vale where Constable painted, a line of trees especially evocative, warranting a sketch, though my efforts could not do it justice.

I rowed to shore and met a couple on the riverbank and asked about the local pub to which I had been recommended. They told me that it had closed down and advised me that it was a few miles to the nearest alternative, though they would be happy to drive me there as they had a holiday house nearby and it was in that direction. When they dropped me off I found vegetables being sold from a stall at the roadside so I chose a fresh sweetcorn and some beans before walking on to the village pub. I had a rest in the recreation field until opening time and then went in. It was sociable and comfortable and they served a generous ham, egg and chips.

I did not stop long before starting on my way back, knowing it was a fair step. All went well until I reached a turn in the road that seemed similar but yet not quite the same. Daylight was fading and things looked slightly different as I turned down a track and found myself amongst unfamiliar fields. I came back and set off down the metalled road instead, but again lost a sense of going in the right direction. When I saw a light, the only one for miles around, I realised I was going to have to seek help despite the time of evening. There was no front door so I had to knock on the window. Imagine the shock of the couple inside, though fortunately they had no curtains drawn and I could see they were watching the rugby. By luck, the man of the house was very kind and unfazed. He asked me if I was trying to get to the jetty. I said yes and he directed me back the way I had come and down the track across the fields.

155

I retraced my steps and headed on down the track. But it was not concrete and I was sure the one I had come along with the elderly couple in their car was concrete. I pressed on for some time but felt I was getting seriously lost. Night had completely fallen, the stars were out and I was heading northeast as I should, but I lost my nerve and turned back. What to do now? It was some way back to the house where I had asked directions. It was much further still to any other possibility of help. I returned to the house and once again knocked on the window, this time in total darkness. The man asked me again where I was heading and we ascertained that it was an old dock I sought and not the jetty, which was up-river. He then very generously drove me down the concrete road to the farm I knew. There was the gate and foot-and-mouth dip. He left his headlights shining down the track and I sensed his concern. He had advised me to take the other track to the jetty because it led right to the river. This way required me to cross two meadows and in the gloom there were no reference points. When the concrete ended at a pad I was faced with alternatives. I turned left. Wrong again. I just avoided going down into a ditch. It would have been an ironic end to be discovered there in the morning. I came back and took the right turn, alongside another ditch and then a pond that I thought I recognised. Finally there was the dock, a strange little block building, derelict and square, hiding its secrets within its drab shape, revealing nothing about its former use.

Kippa was calmly waiting for me at anchor. She was sitting there so patiently, oblivious to my difficulties. I had anchored fore and aft to avoid swinging around and onto the mud at low tide. And there was Rolly tied to the tiny old quay. I struggled down into the dinghy but had no trouble slipping out onto the water once I was seated. It now being slack low tide I had no problem rowing back to the yacht. It was another fine evening and once back on board I was able to chuckle at the absurdity of my latest episode.

48. Butley to Shotley

We didn't mean to go to sea

In the morning Kippa and I pushed downstream against an incoming tide in order to position for an exit from the river just before high tide. We motorsailed close to the edge, making maximum speed over the water and reasonable progress over the ground, by keeping close to the sandy shore where water-skiers were having fun.

As planned, Kippa was hitting the tide just as it slackened a little, but it was still a struggle up the eastern side of the channel, clinging as close as I dared to the spit. Wind was weak and we were motoring hard. Kippa crossed the channel to avoid shallows and then had to come so close she almost touched the stones of the beach as a yacht passed port to port in the narrowest section. In line with the bungalow marked on the chart we were able to strike out to sea. I watched the depth and saw it drop from nine metres to less than three as Kippa crossed the Orford Bar.

At the safe water buoy I was determined to try and sail without motor. Kippa did her best but with a south-easterly some tacking was involved, although on the port tack she could run along the coast at an angle that made good progress. However, on this coast the tide runs awkwardly and only an hour after the flood it turns against you when progressing south. Reasonable progress became slow and then turned into no progress at all until I put the engine on.

We were able to get help from the sails though and needed only a tickover to be able to come close to the wind, at about 35 degrees off it, and make four knots.

There were many yachts appearing as we pushed on beyond the Deben, a river I had wanted to visit but now had to ignore to make my schedule for Shotley. We found ourselves following a larger yacht. I wondered if they knew I had the engine running. If they did not realise, they must have been impressed that Kippa was keeping up.

As we came abeam of Felixstowe the wind was increasing and I could turn off the engine and retain sufficient speed. We beared away at the cardinal post following two other yachts. Approaching the ship channel was like being on the M6 on a Monday morning. The sea was now beginning to cut up and I had to decide where to cross the channel to the recommended yacht track. I chose to make full use of the wind and reach across east to west just after the spit that protects the port of Felixstowe.

Once across, we had wind behind and I chose to lower the main. I calculated that I was safer getting depowered now in case the south-easterly funnelled up more strongly and caused a gybe. It was a bumpy sea we were encountering and Kippa bounced around while the bigger boats appeared to glide through. It might have been a bit over-cautious but under jib alone I was able to cope with the conditions and the traffic.

At Harwich I called the marina and we were obliged to queue for the lift. I enjoyed listening to the professionalism of the marina control's radio operator who was dealing with a mix of tired, impatient and uncertain sailors. I came up to the posts marking the channel to the entrance lock and was called up promptly to enter. As we approached, the wind shivered Kippa in and it took full concentration to get into position alongside without hitting other yachts. Up into the pool, high above sea level, I felt settled in a place I knew and pleased we had made it in time for my friend Guy to join us the next day, despite my getting stuck on the mud and lost in the country.

It was great when Guy arrived. There felt none of the pressure that there had been with other friends on board because I had decided we would just cruise comfortably in the Orwell and Stour and not attempt to complete legs of the voyage. We had an exhilarating sail up the Orwell amongst the many yachts and occasional ship making her way to Ipswich. There had been no shouting on board Kippa for months but when a Flash Harry on port tack tried to run us down I bellowed "Starboard" in my best dinghy-racing voice. It did the trick and we got a contrite look in return.

Guy observed that the size of the sailing boat appeared to be inverse to the competence of the skipper; a small gaff dinghy, perhaps a Mirror, had the most impressive crew, sailing fast without getting in anyone's way.

We found evocative Pin Mill looking its unspoilt best with its house-boats, big old gaffers and traditional boatyard set around the cream-coloured Butt and Oyster pub. We reached the Orwell Bridge and turned round to enjoy a fine sail downstream with the tide now turned. The wind remained blustery and, when approaching an open section before Shotley, I decided it was time to get the main down and continue with jib alone. An oversized yacht with a wideboy Essex skipper passed very close, showing lack of consideration and disdain for slow-coaches. It was with some ungentlemanly amusement that we saw them hit hard by the wind once out of the lee of the trees and lurch away on beam ends to the far shore as they attempted to get some sail down. We oozed past under perfect control, giggling like schoolboys at their predicament. Well, Guy might not have giggled but I certainly detected a smirk. Anyway, that yacht never caught us up from then onwards.

With Kippa back inside the marina, Guy drove me in his car up the road to see Pin Mill at low tide and we spent a most enjoyable evening with a fine pint in the traditional Butt and Oyster inn.

Next day we set off up the Stour beating against a light, pleasant westerly. It gave us a chance to do some fog navigation practice. Guy showed he was well able to judge the tacks and the angle to point to sail the boat well. We nearly went the wrong side of a pole coming in to Mistley where the swans, including some beautiful black ones, were enjoying themselves on a drying bank.

We managed to come against the industrial quay but there were no ladders so we had to climb the wall. Had it been low tide this would have been impossible.

Mistley is either run-down or sparkles with architectural jewels, depending on your viewpoint. Guy pointed out the old Customs House which must have been an important building once upon a time.

We walked through the village and along the riverbank passing oystercatchers, swans, Canada geese and waders. We came to Manning-tree, which was a little more vibrant, sporting more active establishments. Passing over a café which offered no welcome, we turned up a side street to an unspoilt pub, the Red Lion, which had a musty air, and chose a ploughman's lunch. The portions were more than generous and we came away with a doggy bag of cheeses.

On the way back we called in at a health and organic food shop and were tempted by several items. We returned fully laden to Kippa, which we found to be at the top of the quay on the high tide, conveniently placed for stepping aboard. The mudbank was now covered and the swans gone as we slipped down-river, the wind behind us. Picking our way amongst the buoys was easier now and with a reef in we made steady progress. The clouds looked increasingly ominous and, although the wind was not picking up, I felt it best not to risk more sail area. We were soon alongside Parkeston Quay and into the safety of the marina. Then came a sad farewell but we had enjoyed our days together.

About half an hour after Guy left, the storm broke, the wind howled and the rain began to come down. It was nearly two weeks before that weather finally settled.

After a foul night, Juliet came on board in the morning. She was looking forward to the 48-hour crossing to Holland but unfortunately retail therapy at Ipswich had to be prioritised so instead we enjoyed a glass of Vouvray – kindly provided by Guy – before a doubtful excursion to the Bristol Arms, where we tried to outdo each other in getting the publican to treat us as humans not aliens. We both failed, recognising that our interpersonal skills could not defeat a local determined to be rid of us before closing time.

We had a quick peek at Pin Mill and then went on to Ipswich where Juliet dropped me off at the railway station. There was only one day in the next 12 that I could have sailed and that was the day of Simon's 50th birthday party, which I did not want to miss.

49. Shotley to Dover
Great expectations

When settled weather was forecast I returned to Shotley. I had a peaceful night aboard and the next day set off in benign conditions. The sunrise was one of the finest experienced on the trip, lighting up the sky behind Felixstowe with a shocking pink. The port may be commercial but its enormous cranes and vast container ships make a stunning backdrop from one's perch in the marina.

After weeks of planning how to cross the Thames Estuary, I decided on a direct route via the Medusa Channel and Foulger's Gat. I had considered going right out to sea beyond all the shallow dangers but this was not necessary in settled weather. Given more time I would have explored the Essex rivers, Colchester, Maldon and Burnham-on-Crouch. I had even considered going up the River Roach and crossing through the ditch at Havengore, a passage possible only on a high spring tide. That route leads over Maplin Sands and can carry you down with the tide to North Foreland. The difficulty is that it takes three days to get to the River Roach and if you are then confronted by bad weather it has all been pointless. I decided that such exploration would have to wait for another trip.

As Kippa and I came out from the shelter of Felixstowe in convoy with two other yachts, the wind was very light and only motorsailing ensured progress. This was a day when I was content with a light wind because I soon found the sea churning over the shoals, especially in the shallow parts where you cross gaps in the sandbanks to get across to the next channel. I maintained a listening watch on the VTS channels that control shipping, and a sharp lookout, encountering nothing significant until the most southerly of channels where I checked with London VTS, who gave me the all-clear. As I crossed the shipping lane a freighter loomed in the distance, but its speed was not enough to worry me ever though it seemed to take Kippa hours to cross – it was about 90 minutes in reality.

When we approached North Foreland, the shoulder of Kent, the tide turned at last. We had been blessed with excellent speed over ground until then. Now I knew we had to face a foul tide. There was no option. At North Foreland the tides of the Dover Strait and the Thames collide and even without significant wind – it was perhaps a force three easterly at this stage – the sea is a cauldron. I wondered whether to hug the coast or stay out to sea. I decided on the former, able to enjoy a sight of many fine large houses on the clifftops. It was slow going, as expected. I had full sail up and was trying to maximise both the sails and the motor to give me close to five knots over the water. Over the ground I was making 2.5 to three knots. As we crawled along the coast, the speed did drop a little more but eventually we reached Ramsgate with the sea swishing this way and that as the wind increased to a force four east-north-easterly. Fighting the tide, I called the port but found we had to wait, along with other yachts and motor-boats, for a ferry to exit and another to enter. It was a trying time. With little space in the marina I had to get the sails down before entering harbour and the foredeck tossed around as Kippa was left at the mercy of the elements with no directional stability. I motored around to make it more comfortable and then shot in like a rabbit down a hole the moment we were given the go-ahead to enter port. The wind had by now reached force five and I was glad to be in some shelter.

I got off the boat and hunted for better cover in the town. Ramsgate's golden age seemed to be the time when two storeys of arches above the harbour were built. A rather attractive fisherman's church nestles against the wall and, high above, a line of grand houses curves round like a collar.

Beyond those houses lies a block of flats – freshly painted and a signal of an era when civic duty was about housing the poor and not gentrifying the slums. The town centre was disappointing, run-down and lacking purpose. However, on returning to the sea edge, I found a building that looked like an asylum but was in fact an hotel converted into flats. The interesting thing was that it had not been allowed to decay but had been cleverly enhanced by an extension, making the most of what was in fact a building designed by Pugin. In front was a little park and down the slope back to the north-eastern side of the harbour, ignoring the casino, there were creditable efforts to make Ramsgate bearable, most notably a Belgian-style bar staffed with characters from around the world. A cheap vegetarian option was well presented and perfectly digestible. The Ruddles Best bitter was A1.

The next day, with the wind now howling in at force five to six from the east and the rain soaking you to the skin in seconds, I returned to the bar and had a continental breakfast. Sadly they served margarine instead of butter with the croissant, but the coffee was superb.

I took a bus to Broadstairs, which had looked so nice from the sea. From the land it was nothing special, perhaps the continuous rain dampened any prospect. I returned to Ramsgate, shopped in Waitrose and enjoyed home-cooking some organic chicken leg.

The wind died down the next day and the rain stopped. However, the low cloud formed a depressing mist and I did not feel like venturing out. But I did. Once clear of the piers, I assessed the situation. The sea was still unstable and the conditions were unsavoury but I decided I must make the decision based on wind strength and ignore the murk. I put one reef in and was pleased to find Kippa setting off at a good pace with full jib. We threaded our way amongst the buoys along a little channel, finding the beam reach very satisfactory. The sea was not ideal but at least the waves came from the same direction as the wind and once we were clear of the Goodwin Sands things improved. There was enough visibility that if I stayed close to the coast I could see the houses tolerably well. The cliffs at St Margaret's cheered the spirits still further. The wind was dropping so I let out the reef and we continued at a reasonable pace. I was keen to keep sailing as long as possible and with a short passage and a favourable tide Kippa kept on until the water speed finally fell below two knots and the wind gave up just before Dover's eastern entrance. A large ferry was on her way in so I called port control and they advised us to close up and wait instructions. I took down sails close in, seeing the difficulty of doing so within the harbour, and then came right up to a buoy, very close to the wall, and waited for two ferries to come out. When we were given instructions to enter, Kippa and I dived in behind the second ferry, with yet another ferry following in as we dashed across the harbour out of her way. Once inside, the fun continued with a dredger meandering around. Then, with fenders and warps prepared and the marina instructions received after another radio call, we were met by a Speed Ferries catamaran suddenly entering the western side. We followed her and slipped round her stern as she turned into her berth. We finally entered the Granville Dock, pleased to have made it.

With plenty of energy to spare, I went for a walk. Round amongst flyovers and industrial premises, past the old harbour railway station, I clambered up beside a busy road, through a subway to get to the sea side. I climbed a littered and unkempt path deafened by traffic noise roaring below. Further up I was rewarded with a view of a golden strand beside the railway and then Shakespeare Cliff with information panels, then an allotment, then a wooden seat. The path improved and wild flowers took over. I lay down in a slot where it felt the cliff was falling away from the mainland. It was a marvellously private place where nobody could have discovered you, the world tearing past below oblivious to a clifftop hideaway.

From there I made my way across open-access land down to a bridge, beside a council estate with boisterous children who were speaking strong, strange, local accents. They pointed out my path and I rose up amongst the brambles, picking blackberries as I went, noticing a flavour more intense than any I can remember. Everywhere they were abundant and thriving on the chalky outcrop where man had stopped interfering and nature was running riot.

Reaching the ridge-top concrete path, I passed Second World War gun emplacements, then a recently built fort, then around and above an inland part of Dover and finally down a stairway covered in leaves and overgrown by sycamore that could have been Dover's answer to Florentine steps but had become another sign of civic decay.

Beside the busy dual carriageway I found the Flagship, a pub with cordial, unpretentious staff. Apart from the beer delivery, which was all lights and gas, the landlord had got the modern formula right by having great music coming out of a decent sound system and a Wi-Fi that worked well. The big screens played football, but the volume was not intrusive and got turned down when the match ended.

The road outside constantly thundered with traffic but once I was across and back amongst the boats of the harbour it was possible to escape the maelstrom and relax aboard Kippa.

50. Dover to Rye
Rocket ship

Kippa and I set off promptly from Dover to make the most of the tide so that if there was any wind at all we could use it. We motored close to the coast to get some sort of view but the mist almost enveloped Folkestone, and across Dymchurch Bay we were on our own, with nothing in view. The sun did its best to break through and as we closed in on Dungeness I began to see the beach houses. I kept checking for wind and was eventually rewarded with a little southerly. I could not do better than 2.5 knots but, with time in hand, I kept sailing. With a little tide carrying us up to the Power Station and its lighthouses the slow progress gave me the chance to spy the occasional beachcomber or the fishermen working on boats pulled up on the beach. Three fishing boats were at sea, picking out the prawns and other shellfish basking in the warmth of the nuclear outfall. I decided to avoid seafood in Rye!

Once we were past the point the tide continued with us but ever more gently. The wind was dying out and when I recalculated I knew we had to press on under motor in order to enter Rye before high water.

I called the firing range and discovered that live firing was in progress so I steered out to one-and-a-half miles off the coast. This delayed us and by the time we came into Rye Harbour it was not far off high tide. We stopped at the harbourmaster's office, an impressive little building on stilts, in keeping with the surroundings and beautifully decked out. Tying up to the posts was awkward and no help was offered, but the harbourmaster and his assistant were very amenable and wanted to chat. We still had to get up-river to the town so we pushed on as fast as we could, not able to enjoy the setting fully, although the mist had once again become fog. We got as far as a quay that looked like the one shown in a photograph I had seen at the harbourmaster's office so, seeing no reason not to take up a mooring, I moved Kippa into the quay.

She grounded. I got her off but with a worrying splutter from the engine. We got onto the quay a little further back and then I tested the depth with the leadline.

I was not concentrating and started talking to some people in a boat on the opposite side of the river. I was not on the visitors' moorings, they said, but they thought I could get away with staying. They mentioned that where I was it was a hole. I thought no more of this, walked along the quay to investigate the visitor's moorings. They were right by a busy road so when I came back and wondered whether to move on I decided that, as it was now past high water, I might be best not to risk grounding in the river again and instead stay where we were . A bad error as it turned out. As the water dropped Kippa dropped too but when she grounded she began to lean. At first it was not too bad but gradually it got worse. She pulled away further and further from the quay. Worse still, not just the keels but the bow had grounded so the hole she was in became something of a "Thunderbirds" scenario – the episode where the Sidewinder (a forest clearing machine) falls into a pit. It was dark now and I could no longer reach the ladder on the quay so I had supper at an angle. Gradually the situation deteriorated and it felt that if it got any worse Kippa might tip right over. In a fin keeler, drying out is not a good option but at least you refloat upright. In a twin keel, if you fall right over you do not necessarily refloat because the water can enter before you regain buoyancy. I called Sarah and she offered good moral support. I took to my bunk which was now positioned like the cabin of a space rocket. I tried to get some rest but could feel the warps pulling hard. I got up to investigate. Kippa continued to sink into the soft mud, hanging onto the quay and stretching the warps. I now had a difficult decision. Should I loosen the warps or were they the only thing stopping Kippa from tipping over? I decided to loosen them. The stern warp was tight but not too bad. The bow was not so simple. It was now bar tight. The strain on the cleat was obvious and I wondered if I could loosen the rope. I was concerned that if I got my hand caught my fingers would be taken off, or squeezed, with nobody nearby to call for help. I decided I had to risk it.

Taking the rope at a point not too close to the cleat, I yanked. The rope pulled out with a ping and the bow shuddered and slid down the mud. I was left clinging onto the rope waiting for Kippa to slide further. She didn't though. I tied the warp back onto the cleat and wondered what might happen now. Would Kippa continue to slide? Should I let her settle? Where was the hole going? Deeper? Into the channel? I got back into my sleeping bag but did not sleep. I tried to have a pee but the orientation of the boat was so weird I wondered if I had entered the Poseidon Adventure. The floor was now wall and the wall almost ceiling. I thought to myself: "I have had enough adventures, thank you very much." There were times when I wished for a marina, for all their lack of personality. Rye is a beautiful spot and the river is fascinating but at that moment I would rather have been in almost any other harbour.

I got a little slumber and woke several times, not getting back to sleep for long periods. At about four o'clock in the morning I got up and looked out but the river was still very low. Eventually I began to realise I was not in a space rocket any longer. It happened so slowly and without a sound that I could not believe it at first and had to get up to find that the tilt was no longer so bad. Normally you hear some lapping of the water as the tide comes in but drawing off the mud was so gentle that I wondered if I had dreamt it. When I looked up the world was the right way up, the quay was close and Kippa was not complaining.

But would the engine start? I had checked the water filter and it was muddy so during the night I had let out the muddy water and reclosed the sea-cock. Now I opened it again and turned the key. The engine sprung into life as if nothing had been amiss so I decided to try and move down to the visitors' moorings. I pushed Kippa off from the quay without engaging gear. The bow stuck as a little bit of tide drew us forward. I tried pushing off with the boat hook. I tried paddling with the boathook. We got a little further and stopped again. I waited for some more water and then tried again, not risking turning the propeller in case it fouled. Eventually we slipped out into the channel and could engage forward. We turned and gingerly moved up-river. I put the engine back in neutral as soon as we had way on so that if Kippa grounded again she would not be stuck fast. Sure enough, she did ground again. I used the leadline to test depth all around, then backed off where I assessed the best water to be. On the bend there were withies but even in the best part of the channel she grounded.

I looked around. The town was silent, the fog making the neon streetlights disperse their orange glow into a watery splodge. There was no way we could go to sea in this murk, especially with the forecast of fog patches. I waited for more water. When she floated off once more we managed to continue on up to the visitors' quay. We had gone up-river no more than 300 metres in an hour. It was now 5.10 am. High water was predicted at 5.24 am.

51. Rye to Brighton
Beachy Head

I stepped onto shore to confirm it was dry land and to see if Rye was the place I imagined. With pyjama top under a jersey I walked up to the Mermaid Inn, checked the menu for prices and got the usual fright – it is a seriously expensive hideaway. As I walked along the streets, I realised for the first time that in my life the layout of Rye made sense. Until then I had been unable to orientate myself in the town, having previously arrived by car. Rye is a port without the sea and that is why it confuses. It is laid out logically, but from the sea level upwards onto its little hill.

It was still completely dark but when I looked up I saw stars. Stars? In fog? I rushed back down to the boat. I pulled out the almanac. It was now 5.40 am. I checked for the range of tide for the next day. 0.3 metres less. That meant I was going to be in Rye for four days until neap tides had gone by. Engine went on, warps were off and we were on our way in moments. No checklists, still in pyjama top, now with leggings, jersey and lifejacket over the top. I moved Kippa along as fast as I dared, but took it very slowly at the bend where we had encountered most trouble. Could I remember the best route back? We grounded. We backed off. Now what? Abort or carry on? Turn left or right to get better water? I chose the side where there are boats moored to a quay rather than the side where boats were nose into the edge between posts. We got through to the junction of the River Brede, chose the central point and then clung to the side with boats moored against a quay so that if we grounded I might be able to get a warp onto a vessel and perhaps even get to shore if neaped for four days.

We got a little further downstream without grounding so I risked speeding up a little. I looked for buoys and when I saw them and shined a light, reflective tape showed red and green. We got through to the main river just as a fishing boat appeared. I had earlier tried calling the harbourmaster on the VHF in case he was about, it being high tide. A fishing boat had advised me he would not be on duty, perhaps this very boat, because he flashed his deck lights as we passed.

With a wider channel, well marked and with the half-moon shining down, the world was helping Kippa along. Before getting out to sea I took off the warps and fenders but did no more than essentials to be sure to get across the bar. Out over the beach we went, continuing out until the green drying heights on the chart were behind us. At last I could get the boat organised and the sail covers off.

There was a drop of wind and a fine sunrise. Up went the sails and we motorsailed for an hour. At the very earliest moment I turned the engine off. It was a gentle westerly. Happy to tack, knowing the tide was favourable and Eastbourne not far, we glided along. The cliffs before Hastings were very fine and I wondered if Beachy Head would be even more beautiful. I lolled about where a fishing boat was working and eventually the wind died to nothing. We motored on towards Eastbourne. Only for a few minutes was there the slightest wind so I put the tiller pilot on, admired the changing colours in the sky, took in the coast and we made steady progress.

Eastbourne Marina is one of the biggest developments in Britain and yet I liked it. Dense modern housing, but done well. I came through the lock, took up an ideal spot on a pontoon with the warm sun beating down. What joy to be in a marina!

The showers were excellent and so convenient. I spent the afternoon on the boat writing, very content. Later I went over to the yacht club, which I found to be full of London used car dealers – upmarket ones who could afford a motor cruiser. One was sniffing the wine in a way that seemed knowledgeable. As I had discovered before, the motor cruiser types are often a good-natured bunch if you just go along with the ride. They made me welcome and then left me to chomp down a standard bangers and mash followed by a super apple crumble.

I woke at 4.30 am, the body saying: "This is when you normally get up so what is different today?" I tried to explain to myself that we were neither in a hole nor a rocket but safe alongside a pontoon, but the body would not listen and insisted I should get up and do something. I lay in bed until 5.30 and then got up, had a shower and breakfast. Kippa was ready to go into the lock at 6.55 am.

Another sunrise of colours, with clouds shaping aimlessly into smooth ruffles, untroubled by wind from any direction. Yet the sea had swell, so where was that coming from? The east. Under motor Kippa rollercoastered alarmingly. I raised all sail to see if that might create some stability. Gradually I found a gentle north wind working in over Eastbourne, so I switched the engine off and Kippa was soon able to reach 2.5 knots. Once again I was trying to make the most of wind and tide and avoid using the engine so was happy enough, especially on a reach, not tacking. Gradually the wind speed grew and she was up to three and then 3.5 knots.

Beachy Head began with the gentle downs dropping to an insignificant cliff. Then as we continued west-south-west the main cliff opened up. It was far taller and more impressive than the first cliff. The lighthouse appeared, red and white hoops like a tempting sweetie on a stick. With the wind from the quarter, Kippa was broad reaching, almost running. As we began to turn, the boat speed increased a little more and the cliffs opened out to their full grandeur. I moved Kippa in as close as I dared for the finest view of the entire trip. Perhaps the wind was being pushed around the headland because back onto a beam reach it increased to a force five, and Kippa was doing 4.5 to 4.8 knots.

The wonder continued as the Seven Sisters unravelled before us like pure white cotton sheets. A gentle undulation of the land had been sliced by the sea again and again over the years, keeping the Sisters' faces clean. I counted them. There were eight! Perhaps there were seven originally and the eighth appeared recently.

Further on there were more gorgeous cliffs, still white but now with a topping like a soft pale praline chocolate. After Beachy Head comes Birling Gap, bringing back happy memories despite the café there being a run-down greasy spoon establishment waiting to fall in the water. Later the cliffs separate at Cuckmere Haven: more happy memories of cycling with the children. Beyond is Alfriston, set in a valley of seclusion and peace. Perhaps in ten thousand or a million years Alfriston will fall into the sea. Property prices should hold up for a while yet. Gradually the cliffs got lower as we came towards Brighton and the settlements grew.

Picking out further landmarks, I noted the black windmill. I had been expecting white weatherboarding and felt slightly cheated for some reason. Then I felt sorry for the windmill as it sat forlornly in a cultivated field with a busy road passing below. Its end will surely come before Alfriston and, when it does, perhaps it will burst into flames in a howling gale that sparks its sails before it falls into the sea with a frightful hiss.

I looked for Brighton Pier but curiously it was not obvious. I find perspective and distance at sea very deceptive, a light shining 20 miles away can seem close, while a large structure like a pier can disappear into the background at only two miles off, even on a clear day.

I kept sailing right up to the breakwaters, taking down the sails only at the last safe moment allowing for tide and muck-ups. There was none that day. It was an exceptional passage and a rare treat.

52. Brighton to Poole

Scooper sailing

The marina at Brighton is good. I rather like the fashionable development of restaurants that overlook the harbour, although the dwellings go on for too long and lack the cohesive sense achieved at Eastbourne.

Walking through a rather unpleasant carpark behind the main development, I searched for the electric train. It stopped in September. Funny really. Stopped at the end of summer, I suppose, and the temperature this day was probably at least 21 degrees. I considered the bus but was attracted by all the Regency villas on the other side of the main road. I climbed up into Kemp Town, which is a wonderful suburb; trapped between bohemian and stylish, the area could only be part of Brighton. Inside the buildings one might find enormous wealth – or students scraping a living.

The shopping street that runs parallel to the seafront is very eclectic going from music to ethnic to motor parts to antiques, each shop has that Brighton eccentricity. In the music shop the owner commented that he hates cellos. He said so as if they were a political party he loathed. Another shop was selling unusual and original pies. When I tried to buy one, the assistant was busy with something else. Not rude, just busy with a more important conversation with someone in the back of the shop. As I walked on I searched for a particular delicatessen and café I remembered. After passing almost every kind of shop one could imagine, I found the place. Sadly it had changed. Perhaps changed hands. Nevertheless, I sat down and ordered a cake and tea. The cake was inedible – left too long in a packet and then left out too long: cardboard flavour and texture. I decided to risk mentioning it. I was not kicked out but instead it was willingly changed for something more palatable.

People were coming in and out, men with dangling and grunge

T-shirts, unshaven and unwashed, women over-made-up with characterful but not pretty faces, wearing semi-provocative, faintly kinky clothes. It was as if fashion were non-fashion. Anything as long as it's not black, though it could be black. Artistic but not crafty. Creative on a shoestring.

People seemed to be ordering a house special. A salad box. So I did too. Five portions, but then you could add houmus and yoghurt, they did not count apparently. The assistant to whom I had complained earlier bore no grudge and was keen to ensure that I got a really full box with as many goodies as possible. She had been moaning to her colleague but now she seemed to have grown friendly since serving some customers. It seemed that she may have appreciated that I had tried to be polite and very English in the way I had mentioned the cake problem. Not put off by cultural and language difference, she was Polish perhaps, and her reaction was not an English one, more a sense of needing time to warm to a customer. Having travelled around Britain I found it revealing to speak to other Europeans and see just how different they are from us all in the UK.

The overall impression of Kemp Town is of West London encapsulated in a few streets. Edge, variety, diversity, friendliness, danger, risk and reward. These people are into pleasure, into community support, utterly open to new ideas, rehashing the old ones mercilessly to earn another bob.

From Brighton I had three options, Shoreham, Littlehampton or Chichester. I aimed for Littlehampton but kept my options open in case the weather changed. With the wind coming from the east-north-east, Kippa and I broad-reached out away from shoals and rocks, then gybed back into the coast to get some view of Hove and beyond. I decided that Shoreham would be too industrial and too short a hop, even though with a light wind progress was slow. I had tons of tide in hand for Littlehampton but not enough water speed for Chichester. I tried to sail all the way but finally we were left with a few miles to go and the tide about to turn. I had made a good stab at sailing all the way but reality had to kick in. At the rate Kippa was progressing we were not going to get there before 10 pm. Simon had rung to say he was coming down so I put the engine on and motored. It was about 5 pm when we came up the River Arun. I moored Kippa to the wrong place on the town quay and was shoved off, but not unpleasantly, by a tourist boat. He pointed out the sign but did not have a go and showed patience, which I thought was extremely reasonable. I caused mayhem along the pontoon as we rafted up outside, but everyone took it in their stride and was helpful. Kippa ended up alongside a pretty boat with wooden topsides and a woofly little hound called Harry. He looked as if he had escaped from the Scrubs but perhaps he was a pedigree that never caught the public imagination.

Simon duly arrived on time and we dived into Wetherspoons, full of quite other beings than those in Brighton. Mostly youngsters, now done up in their Friday night gear. The girls were making it very obvious they were available, while the lads pretended they didn't care. It was as if the females were having to try extra hard for an unimaginative set of males.

Simon, Kippa and I were blessed with a glorious day for the passage from Littlehampton to Gosport. The wind was light again but with the scooper sail and lots of tide we made reasonable time. We had to reach out a couple of times but eventually we settled on a good course that took us through the Looe Channel. At last Simon could enjoy some steering. He had to master Kippa, which was new to him, learning to avoid the gybe while maintaining a good course. He managed it and had Kippa on a steady track beyond Selsey Bill. Unfortunately the wind died out and although he persisted to the bitter end, we eventually had to put motor on for the last third of our journey to Gosport.

The boats in the Royal Clarence marina dwarfed Kippa. There were round-the-world yachts, ocean racers, and a "yacht" the size of a small ship which was more a private hotel than a motor cruiser – the toy of a mega-rich owner who probably only spends the odd weekend on board. The navy, customs, police and the ferries all combine to create a hive of activity where everyone goes about their business briskly. Kippa felt very small in the scheme of things but not insignificant to me.

Back to single-handed from Gosport and with only a parsley plant and a stuffed dog for company, Kippa and I headed off for Lymington. On checking the speed over ground, I found that Kippa was doing 6.5 knots. Remembering that the tide rips past Cowes, I realised we were in for a fast passage. The visibility was moderate but it was nice to see the familiar landmarks along the coast of the Isle of Wight. After Cowes we crossed the Solent towards Lymington. The speed was terrific, so I dug out the almanac and made some fresh calculations. I reckoned Poole was on the cards, with possible tidal streams of 4.4 knots at Hurst Point. I adjusted the course and pushed on past Lymington and Yarmouth. The sea swirled but, with not a drop of wind, there was not a wave to be seen. Even the shingle bank had no white water. Kippa tore past The Needles, which looked more like decayed teeth in a gaping mouth, and out into Christchurch Bay. We passed a coaster coming up the channel and I gave them a wave. They gave a cheerful wave back from the bridge and I saw she was registered in Hull. Had they been Kippa'd before perhaps? Out into Christchurch Bay I expected some swell or some wind but there was nothing. It was almost a millpond. The sun began to break through to provide a glimpse of Christchurch in the distance.

It was no time at all before we reached Studland Bay and were turning into the channel. A small ship was led out by a pilot and then powerboats churned up the calm sea, making unnecessary waves that unsettled us as we made our way into harbour. The fortified house on Brownsea Island looked very fine and Kippa followed a Hunter Horizon up the channel. We diverged and Kippa overtook, almost getting out of channel when I spotted the cardinal mark just in time. It was a straightforward arrival into the town quay marina, apart from yet another gin palace on steroids making move waves than a supertanker.

53. Poole to Teignmouth
Jurassic Coast

My main concern on this early October trip was being blown out of the water. We kept off the Lulworth range and thought we had cleared the problem when I heard a call from the warship Somerset, telling vessels to keep ten miles away as they were live firing. The coastguard checked and she was in the next bay, so I could stop worrying and search for Durdle Door, a stone arch west of Lulworth Cove. The visibility was not good enough to make out the coastal shapes, though the colours made the trip a pleasure.

Weymouth was a straightforward entrance and then we curved through the town to a lifting bridge into the marina. The following morning there was not a breath of wind and the forecast predicted calm for the entire day so I decided to go walking as there was no sailing to be done. I took the bus that runs along Chesil Beach and jumped out after about 15 minutes. The fields stretched down to the Fleet, a little inland sea behind the pebble bank. The paths were well trodden and the hedges full of interesting plants. Down by the water, which is slightly tidal, the serenity was complete. Chesil Beach protected this haven for birds and there was a sense that man had been stopped from spoiling the tranquillity.

I made a short stop at a very rural country hotel hoping for a cup of tea but nothing appeared so I walked on and discovered a tiny chapel covered in lichen. Inside it was utterly plain, no pews, just a few chairs facing out from the walls. The altar was hardly more than a dining table decoration but the effect was of complete retreat from the tribulations of life. The churchyard was equally calm, the dead having been buried with love and without pageant.

I walked up the hill again, past some pretty cottages at East Fleet and then found a bus to take me back to Weymouth.

It had taken until Ramsgate before I believed I could complete the circumnavigation. This was the first time I was not chasing a schedule; my only commitment was to meet Tom and then take an exam but there was still another week to go for that. The final hurdle was Portland Bill, a significant tidal race, but in the benign conditions we were having I foresaw no problem.

Taking care to obtain all local advice, Kippa and I set out along the peninsula from Weymouth to the rocky outcrop of the island of Portland, famous for its stone. There was plenty to see and a little sailing too. We had left in good time so that Kippa could take advantage of any wind there was and not have to motor.

The old railway track was clearly visible on the eastern side and then I saw the fine structure of the lighthouse. I had been told that one could sail so close in that the top window of the lighthouse was just above an obelisk by the rocks. Sure enough, the route was there to be followed and Kippa sailed safely off the rocks in deep water but avoiding the race. We had experienced a slightly uncomfortable sea just before the point but, as we passed the transit of the monument with the lighthouse, the water was slack and calm. Timing was perfect and as we came out to the western side, the tide was with us and increasing to sweep Kippa along the Chesil Beach towards our next port – our final port before the finishing line.

I relaxed and enjoyed the view of Dorset. A little misty, but that made the church on the hillock by Abbotsbury even more Thomas Hardy. We passed West Bexington, a village that runs like a ribbon down the hillside and then came upon the distinctive sandy-coloured cliffs by Bridport. The sun was out and it was reasonably warm, bringing out beachcombers and autumn holidaymakers.

Bridport turned out to be a troublesome harbour with a most dreadful swell, even though the wind was light and the sea no more than slight. On a loose plastic pontoon, Kippa tossed about like a maverick at the rodeo. I couldn't get off quickly enough.

I went down to the pub and watched some rugby, hoping things might improve by the time I came back, but in fact things were worse. It was almost impossible even to climb aboard the bucking bronco. There was absolutely no way that I would get any sleep on board so I went to look for a bed and breakfast, not expecting to have much luck. The inn by the harbour was hellish expensive but an old hotel offered an adequate room at a fair price and, as it was now 10.30 pm, I jumped at the chance.

From Bridport to Teignmouth was a fair distance, about 27 nautical miles, but it was all good sailing. If only more legs could have been this way. When I came out of the harbour another boat with a crew that I had met the night before took photographs of Kippa with Golden Cap in the background. Then we sailed in tandem along the coast, though Kippa could not quite keep up.

The cliffs were beautiful all the way and there were things to look out for throughout the voyage, including the wreck of the famously looted Napoli near Sidmouth. When I saw the entrance to the Exe I could also make out Dawlish and Teignmouth. I chuckled to think of how far it had seemed with Becky just from Starcross on the Exe to Teignmouth. Now it was just a piece of a much longer leg that did not feel particularly far. I had reached a stage where I could be in Kippa as long as I wished with the only limitation being the weather. I could even go without sleep for 18 hours and not be bothered.

We formally crossed the line of the outward journey as we came to Teignmouth. There were no cheers, no boats to greet us, no flags waving. It was a quiet moment of reflection and the strangest-ever feeling. The feeling that we could go on and round again. It was ridiculous, my having wanted to give up several times along the way, but I could have turned Kippa south and headed for Brixham and then on, even to France the next day. It is a weird sensation to complete a circumnavigation. It was not a sense of relief for me. It was a quiet sense of satisfaction in one way, but sad in another.

For celebration I settled for calling Becky on the mobile phone and telling her where I was. She vividly remembered the place and the moment we had shared. Later I called Monica and then I called Sarah, who had played such a crucial role in helping me carry on.

I had hoped to find Captain Platt at Teignmouth but he had left and the atmosphere was not the same. I felt a stranger in a foreign land when I should have been coming home. I suppose I wanted to say to the harbourmaster "Here I am again."

54. Teignmouth to Torquay
The Exam

A minor motivation to circumnavigate Britain was to prove to myself and others that I could sail a yacht tolerably well. I failed my Yachtmaster exam in 2005 – which was what I had expected, with my limited experience – but the episode demonstrated that people did pass the exam with flaws in their ability. I felt that if they could pass, so should I be able to, despite my own limitations which are laziness, lack of attention to detail, poor memory, slowness to take things in, lack of physical strength and stamina, lack of practical skills and so on and so forth!

I can generally bring together a group and encourage teamwork, however, going solo for most of the trip tested a zone within me I had not explored and this was perhaps the most fascinating mental examination. It took me to my limit of endurance and perseverance. Several times I felt like giving up and, after crossing the Irish Sea a second time, I determined I definitely would give up. It was only the calmness and gentle encouragement of Sarah that had helped me to focus on what I had achieved that then spurred me on to have another go.

Even at Penzance I had severely questioned the sense of the undertaking and it had taken the friendship and good sense of Keith to encourage me round Land's End and recover my momentum.

I had wondered whether I should attempt the Yachtmaster exam again. I feared failure. I feared an examiner would pick holes but not see the bigger picture.

It was a requirement of the examination that there was a crew and I reckoned that Tom was my first choice. Tom is a tough, resilient character who does not get flustered easily. He is happy as crew and is not a skipper second-in-command. Fortunately he was willing and able, indeed keen, to spend a few days aboard around the exam.

Less fortunately for Tom, his car broke down while he was kayaking in Devon, but he still managed to get a lift to Teignmouth so as not to let me down.

On the first evening we went out and had a look at the navigation lights of the entrance. I was pleased to see that Tom's steering was now more accurate. Recent experience had been of benefit.

The day before the exam, a Tuesday, the wind blew up and the rain lashed down. I decided that any practice would be counter-productive and it would be better to take it easy. We had a game of Scrabble which I just won. On later days Tom would beat me easily and then completely slaughter me, scoring a bonus 50 for putting down all his letters in one go.

Gradually I had been able to settle down into a quietly confident mood, taking the attitude that if I did not pass, it was more their problem than mine. I knew I would make mistakes and have gaps in my knowledge. I was never going to pass with distinction. What I had to concentrate on was not making a stupid mistake.

I had also decided to sail as I would normally. The only exception to this would be that I would manage the boat more than I might normally. With crew on board, I like to give them a chance to share in the management but I sensed that most sailing skippers are quite traditional in their hierarchical approach.

I met Paul, the examiner, at Polly Steps where Teignmouth Corinthian Yacht Club keep their boats. Immediately Paul said that he was expecting to be met by boat. I did not allow this to faze me and just shrugged a little and did not attempt to justify or explain. We walked round through the town where I had left the dinghy, in what I felt was the sensible place, just a short row from the pontoon where Kippa was. I sensed Paul was on his guard now as I knocked an oar into a boat at the mooring. Again I did not allow myself to be fazed and reacted to it without making a meal of such a tiny thing.

We got on board and I felt that Tom was doing his bit, taking Paul's mind off my imperfect start to the day. Preliminaries of paperwork went better. He took note of my experience without making anything of it. I also played it down.

We were soon cast off, turning Kippa between the pontoons. It was a tight gap and I wondered if the tide would catch us out. I boosted revs and we shot out into the main channel before tide could take over. We went out of the harbour and I raised sail with Tom at the helm.

Things were going well. The sun was out, there was a little wind and we were sailing along. I felt good. A large ship in the distance made me wonder whether it was a ship or the Ore Stone, an island. Referring to it as the Battlestar Gallactica, Paul seemed amused and was beginning to relax.

When we started to slow down, Paul criticised the lack of a genoa and asked if I had a spinnaker. I said I did have a scooper sail and asked if he would like me to put it up. I asked if he would mind helping to take it down if the wind got up. He was fine with this and so, although I had previously thought it best not to risk the scooper during the exam, now I was going for it.

Preparations and raising the scooper went well, Paul offering assistance. Kippa picked up speed and I felt points were being racked up. Paul realised I knew how to use the sail and was not afraid of it.

Tom steered a very good course, kept quiet and boosted the points still further. I wondered if perhaps positives were outweighing earlier negatives by now.

We took down the scooper to do some exercises, the first of which was Man Overboard. Without warning Paul put the horseshoe buoy and light into the water. I saw him do it, fortunately, being at the companion way just as he did it with his back to me. I think he had thought I was down below, not aware of what was happening on deck. I jumped into action, took the tiller and made the radio call myself.

I had Tom get the boathook while I put the engine on. I had expected Paul to require me to do it without motor but he left me to it. I was not quite sure of which strategy to adopt but Kippa helped me out as she spun round and jumped at her horseshoe. We passed close as Tom got prepared, we spun again and Tom went for it. He could not get a hold. We had missed. Kippa spun again and I told Tom it was my fault and that I would get into wind better. We came alongside perfectly but poor Tom could not get hold of it. I took the boathook and made a desperate lunge, sensing failure was upon us. The horseshoe rose up and into Kippa, gliding through the air as if on wings. I certainly had little to do with it. But had we done enough or were we now on the slippery slope?

The next problem was to sail to a GPS position. This tested my ability to steer a course as well as my wind awareness. It went well and we were on a reasonable track. I was keen to get this little test spot-on and chose to heave to against the tide so that we could hit the spot and remain on it for a while. With Tom's help and a kindly wink from the gods, we got it right, the jib even holding to windward on its track. I admitted to Paul this did not happen by design, it was just a lucky break. I hoped that the frankness would play well. I think it did.

On we went around the Ore Stone to the next test – find a rock. We had to use a transit and I was unable to guess which one Paul was referring to. I am not sure that getting it right would have counted any more than getting it wrong. He could tell I understood the principles of transits and of depth. The answer he was looking for was a road. This really depended on local knowledge and was distinctly obscure. It was the type of problem that examiners set wanting the examinee to fail so that they can prove their superior knowledge. He was chuffed to find I could not guess the answer and took pleasure in revealing it. However, we did find the rock and he was happy that I understood the concept of a search pattern. He had settled into a mode of thinking: "This guy knows the basics and can apply them. He is nothing special but he is not a fool either." I sensed things were just starting to swing in our favour. It was about ensuring that I did not fail now.

The next problem was to anchor. He asked me to choose an anchorage, which I did. He asked me about holding, the sea-bed and this time I was able to answer confidently. Anchoring fascinates me because it is a vital part of traditional and modern seamanship. I read the chart correctly, guessing a small "f" to be fine on the basis that a small "c" was coarse. We sailed in and I chose a depth of five metres. The boat slowed to zero on the counter but still had 5.8 metres of depth. I hung the anchor in the water and saw that the water was flowing past the chain. I decided to wait and let the sea gods do the business. Kippa was still moving and gradually she was slowing up completely. When Paul called five metres from the cockpit, Kippa had just stopped moving. I let the anchor down as if it was how I had planned it. Tom held the boom out and we dropped back as the anchor started to bite. It had gone like a dream. We were definitely ahead now.

A quick sandwich and a drink and we were off again, sailing between the Lead Stone and the Ore Stone. I was keen to capitalise on the positive atmosphere and wanted to show I had the confidence to take this route. I was trying to notch up points for tidal awareness and boat management. When Tom got tired I took over. The wind gods did their bit and we sped along, getting up to 4.8 knots, chatting away, Paul now telling us about his fast boat and his wide range of experience.

He had very fairly told me that pretend fog might descend so I was ready when the test came. We discussed the problem and I seemed to come up with an answer he liked. I knew this was my strong suit. I actually enjoy this test because it gives you a chance to show you understand tides and compass bearings. It is spatial navigation and I am just about able to hold a picture of where I am in the world in my head.

We tacked into the coast to pick up a depth where the target buoy would lie, further up the coast. I checked the tidal depths with reference to a curve. Paul saw me do this, questioned my workings and was happy. He was encouraging me on.

We tacked at the right depth and the wind gods slowed us down so that there was no panic. We eased up the coast. I was not able to determine arrival at the buoy precisely but Tom later said that the direction was so accurate that we were on collision course when Paul said OK.

Coming into the harbour, I was about to take the sails down – but this was a major error, putting up and taking down sails outside harbour.

Inside the harbour we picked up a buoy and then came onto the pontoon. I began to let things slip, throwing a rope in the water. I did not panic, though I was getting nervous that earlier success was now being whittled away.

Down below came a test on lights and shapes and I struggled badly on some quite tricky ones. But by then Paul had made up his mind and so he showed me some easy ones so he could tick the box, describing my ignorance as being rusty, which was generous.

A passage plan for a long voyage that I had prepared earlier seemed to satisfy him and the associated chart work was fine. He had seen that my charts were bang up-to-date and this scored well. He seemed to sense that despite the rough edges I had most of the important things cracked.

When he asked me how I felt the day had gone I was noncommittal. When he said "These are the things I did not like" I felt hopeful and, sure enough, he said he would recommend me for a pass. He realised I was well aware of my limitations and would always have much to learn. I have found as time goes by that in sailing I discover more about what I do not know and the breadth of new learning grows.

Tom had done a great job, not putting a foot wrong. He had said all the right things, followed instructions and mentioned a problem only when it was a problem, letting me sort everything else out.

55. Teignmouth to Topsham

Dressing up

With the exam over and the circumnavigation completed, I might have felt deflated. Or elated. Probably somewhere in between. Or somewhere different. One thing was clear-cut, I did not want to make a stupid sailing mistake now so we did everything by the book. We raised sail inside the harbour, as advised, and saw a man watching us intently on the spit. I am sure he wasn't, but we imagined he was spying for the examiner, checking we really did what we were told. Once past the point, the secret agent seemed satisfied as Tom and I sailed gently away. It was a simple crossing to the River Exe but not so simple an entrance; the navigation marks are hard to read and we spent ages staring at monuments, churches, buoys and anything else we could identify and correlate with the chart. No one mark could be identified with complete certainty but eventually we agreed on where we were and then found the channel buoys and the cardinal mark; not the yellow and black object we first saw, which was the flag of a fisherman's lobster pot. We threaded our way along the winding channel to the marina and spent the evening at a Chinese restaurant to celebrate before continuing on up the River Exe the next morning.

The final day on Kippa brought fine sunshine. The northerly direction of a gentle wind did not allow us to sail up-river more than one reach so it was under motor that we arrived at Topsham. Just as we sought out a spot to land I saw the tower of the bed and breakfast I had booked for Sarah and Joanna to stay with me for the following night. A ramp by the river was perfectly sited to unload so we gingerly went out of the channel across to it, hoping for sufficient depth. As we trickled across, the depth fell away and I decided it was too risky. We touched but got off quite easily.

We continued up the channel to the main quay, only to ground on the way in, just short of a narrow boat. I was concerned that we might waste yet more time grounding so I got into the dinghy and rowed, towing Kippa behind me. Being a tug was fun and Kippa was led along by her lead this way and that to get round a mudbank until at last we got to a deeper patch alongside a rib. Tom and I clambered across to tie up, then I dashed to the bed and breakfast with my bags. I ran back and we were off up-river again to find Retreat Boatyard. The channel funnelled out and then turned and narrowed to follow close to the bank. Finally we reached the trot moorings, a series of buoys tied in a line. We made a meal of tying up but were keen to satisfy ourselves that all was secure. We had a snack, rowed across to the yard and booked in.

Tom's car was still not repaired so he spent the night on the boat while I discovered Reka Dom, Russian for house by the river, and its tower, which has uninterrupted 360-degree views, fitting for a circumnavigator to contemplate a trip of a lifetime round his home island.

I still wished we had been able to go round the top of Scotland but knew that had Kippa and I pressed on northwards from Arisaig, I might never have completed the voyage. If we had reached Cape Wrath when the strong northerlies blew in, we might well have been forced to turn back. Abandoning until the following summer might have been the result. It had been right to head back south, enjoy Eigg, Muck and Loch Sunart with Ashley before limping through the Caledonian Canal to Inverness. Getting Kippa sorted at Caley Marine had been essential and set us on the road home. As time went by and the weather improved from Amble southwards, confidence grew and speed increased, enabling Kippa to get home in one piece, while I enjoyed the balmy autumn and completion of the circuit, arriving fit and able to contemplate another adventure.

A couple of days later saw the final celebration. Dave and Sue Rolfe, as well as Gordon and Sue Davidson, who had kindly made the long trip down from Worcester, joined us for a grand Sunday lunch at the Lighter Inn in Topsham. Afterwards we went up-river to see Kippa at her final mooring place. The last moments on board my little ship were spent, very fittingly, with Dave Rolfe who dressed Kippa with flags from stem to masthead to stern so that photos could be taken in the fading light of a pale, watery sunset.

Appendix A
Safety equipment on board

Having chosen a reasonably priced yacht, I had the budget available to equip well. I did not buy top of the range every time – for example I compromised on the liferaft, considering it a final back-up, but I did buy a very good chartplotter as a first line of defence. I decided against buying an EPIRB which is a device that will activate and send a distress signal if you fall in the water. It seemed too large to be practical to wear. There is a new system which is smaller but I discovered it only at the last moment before leaving Falmouth and decided it was too late to investigate thoroughly. On another similar trip I would certainly research the system where you have a tag on your person and when that tag leaves the proximity of a beacon on the boat the distress signal activates.

I had no emergency steering device on board and I had no manually operated steering device either. With a larger boat I would certainly fit one of these. If I had lost the rudder then I would have been down to using sails and trailing ropes to get any control. Although I can sail a dinghy rudderless, whether I could have sailed Kippa rudderless using the sails to get steering is doubtful. I certainly doubt I could have done it accurately enough to enter a harbour, but I think there is a chance I could at least have kept off a coast, or made headway towards shelter and help. Perhaps without the rudder the dynamics of a twin keel make rudderless sailing impossible. I do not know.

I chose three Crewsaver lifejackets with light, hood and crotch straps At first I did not bother with a crotch strap but later I followed Tom's example. It was more of a fiddle when I took clothes off but I soon got used to it, like wearing a seatbelt. The lifejacket lights I chose were not automatic. I found some Italian-designed ones called C-light that I liked because they were easy to turn on and off, even with very cold hands.

They seemed robust and were easy to maintain. However, you have to be careful how the lid is screwed back on. I found it necessary to check the operation of the light carefully after replacing or checking batteries.

1 also had one Seago lifejacket in case there was a fourth person on board and we were just pottering around the harbour. Although it conforms to the normal safety specifications it is probably not of the quality of the Crewsaver. Indeed, during maintenance in the winter when I came to check the manual inflation it did not want to inflate through the tube on the first couple of attempts. On the third attempt it did inflate fine and I assume the valve was just a little stuck.

I fitted the jackstays, lines running up the sides of the deck, because I liked to clip on a harness whenever I got out of the cockpit onto deck. I was just as diligent in calm weather as rough.

Interestingly, the previous owners had no liferaft on board so although I bought only a basic model, at least I had one, and it did conform to proper standards.

Kippa has a radar reflector but I was always aware that it is not visible to many radars.

I kept an emergency boarding ladder in the cockpit locker.

Down below, Kippa had two fire extinguishers, a fire blanket, a first-aid kit, a first-aid manual and a survival bag.

I did not have a grab bag but instead got in the habit of using a haversack. This served as a grab bag which could be taken to a liferaft in an emergency and would normally have money, credit cards, mobile phone and a small bottle of water in it.

During the trip I also purchased an "Oscar", which is a man-overboard sling on a rope.

Appendix B
Navigational and electrical equipment

I learnt to navigate with paper charts and it was only recently that I started to use a Global Positioning System. For this journey I was tempted to manage with just a handheld GPS but when I saw what a chartplotter can do I felt it was a very worthwhile device, particularly as I was single-handed for most of the journey.

Kippa was already equipped with a handheld GPS which also connected to a Yeoman Plotter. A good way of combining paper charts with a GPS, the Yeoman Plotter was my back-up. The chartplotter I chose was the Navman 5505i with full UK coverage charts. Dave and Sue Rolfe had fitted one and I had read that the Navman was more intuitive than most devices, and so it proved. Under pressure when there was an extra function I wanted to explore, I never got angry with the unit, but would always find what I was looking for, such as the anchor alarm.

The distance and speed log with depth sounder was a standard unit. The most important thing I learnt about it was not to antifoul the sensor in the keel!

The VHF radio was a Standard Horizon which came with a cockpit microphone. The unit failed in Bridport and the problem was never identified. The cockpit microphone jammed on occasionally and I never had full confidence in the unit. It was easy to use and when it worked, it worked well. An old Simrad that John Rice lent me was completely reliable and although less fancy, I would always prefer a unit that is 100% reliable.

The handheld VHF radio, also Standard Horizon, worked

reasonably well but its transmitting power and aerial meant that it was limited in range.

The autopilot was a Simrad. It worked well when the connection was good, but when it was poor it was a real nuisance and I had to keep fixing and cleaning the brass pin and socket. The Clipper Navtex for collecting weather information was very reliable. Occasionally we were out of range and did not get the signal but in general it proved its worth. I actually did not completely understand how to use it until about Lindisfarne!

I also carried:

Bretton plotter
Dividers
Pencils
Rubber
Hand bearing compass
Binoculars with internal compass
Small binoculars
Small battery charger
Six AA rechargeable batteries, six for lifejacket lights, two spare
Four AAA rechargeable batteries (three for headlight)
Two D rechargeable batteries for large torch
Spare AA and AAA batteries
Laptop computer (Panasonic)
Torches
Stereo
Shaver
Hairdryer
Ammeter
Headlamp

Electrical dinghy pump, which decided it did not want to go sailing and jumped overboard on my first attempt to use it.

Appendix C
Sailing equipment

Mainsail (the mainsail of Kippa has a packaway cover that is kept on the boom at all times. There are two reefs for the mainsail which are controlled from the cockpit.

Jib (with a furler so you can roll it up)
Scooper sail (for light winds)
Winch handle (I bought a spare on the advice of Morris)
Leadline (to measure depth and check whether the sea-bottom was sand, mud, shells or rock)
Main anchor (CQR type)
Hand start handle for the engine, not that I had the strength to crank the engine by hand
Folding ladder
Two large fenders, three small fenders
Warps (ropes for tying to the quay or pontoon)
Black ball, to show when Kippa was anchored
Cone to show we were motorsailing, which the examiner noticed was very new and obviously been used very little. Red face!
Boathook
Long and small brush
Bucket and sponge
Kedge anchor (Danforth)

On the rail I had a big round fender which Becky and I called Globo. but it got lost over the side at The Lizard so I bought a new one which was just the right size to fit in the locker. It was a great thermometer because when the air was cold you could take it straight out of the locker but when it was hot it expanded and you had to pull hard to squeeze it out of the locker. In 2007 it was always easy to get it out, even in mid- summer! The outboard motor for the dinghy was stored on a bracket on the cockpit rail.

In the stern cockpit locker I kept a petrol can, two-stroke oil, a diesel can, a diesel fill funnel, a measuring jug and some green stuff that you put with diesel to stop bacteria growing.

I bought four backrests to clip onto the guardrails but lost one over the side during the voyage.

I carried a spare impeller and a spare filter for the engine.

Appendix D
Maintenance and miscellaneous equipment

I carried two toolboxes, one with screwdrivers, pliers, wrenches and assorted items, and the other with wire wool, wire brushes, electrical wire, string, duck tape, glue, Sellotape and suchlike. I also carried a Swiss army knife, a box of mini-screwdrivers, a tube of crack repair and a dinghy repair kit.

After I had accidentally thrown the electrical dinghy pump in the water I used the manual dinghy pump and found it to be perfectly satisfactory, just a bit of exercise. For insurance reasons I had a cycle lock for the outboard motor.

I found Mer polish good for keeping the hull nicely polished and used Renovo to waterproof the sail covers and the sprayhood, though all of the waterproofing products I used did their job.

At a later date I also bought a vernier gauge which was useful to measure the size of nuts and bolts. I had a dustpan and brush and clothes pegs on board.

I carried travel games to entertain the crew but only one was used and that was with Tom, who nearly always beat me at Scrabble.

I had a big, reliable, simple alarm clock which was easy to read at any time.

I dropped a bag in the water at Padstow and that wrecked my Nokia mobile phone so I bought a cheap Sony Ericsson in Morrisons in Bideford. It used up its battery more quickly but otherwise was fine. I was on pay-as-you-go with Vodafone and it was very expensive and the customer service was infuriating, so I used landlines where possible.

I used a Nikon digital camera, which was troublesome and too slow so that I missed many snaps. When there was time to set up the shot, the quality was fine.

I carried Post-it Notes which I used to mark pages in the almanac or the pilot book, as well as notes to myself, such as lists or reminders.

I carried a tarpaulin just in case I needed some extra weather protection. It came in useful when sorting out things on a pontoon.

I also had a box of visiting cards printed I could give to people I met.

Appendix E
The galley

Equipment and materials around the galley included:

disinfectant	wash kit
bread knife	insulated bag
small sharp knife	coasters
sharp serrated knife	matches
can opener	mats
bottle opener	cocktail sticks
plastic cups and plates	chopping board
cutlery	fish slice
kettle	plastic boxes
saucepans	cutlery
frying pan and lid	wooden spoon
oven dish	black refuse bags
lighters	plastic bags
scissors	kitchen roll
glasses	foil

I bought two large water containers in case there was a problem with the main tank as well as various small water bottles. Boiled water from the main tank was adequate but tea and coffee tasted better with the freshest water from a refilled mineral water bottle.

I also had a couple of spare plastic bottles (very clearly marked) that I kept in the cockpit locker. One crew member, whose standards in such matters are higher than mine, did not want to know about this but I found them very useful when Kippa was in rough seas because it was a convenient way to pee without going below, which can be distinctly awkward. Another crew member asked for a larger capacity, which he had no problem filling, and another complained that the size of the neck was insufficient, even though they were smoothie bottles with a wide neck – but I just told him to stop boasting!

Appendix F
Charts and books

The most useful book on board was the "Reeds Almanac". It is packed with masses of information plus, by using the monthly updates, you can plan with a fair degree of confidence, although one piece of information that was often imprecise or inaccurate was the cost of staying in a harbour or marina. The first pilot book I used was Mark Fishwick's "West Country Cruising Companion", which has well structured guidance. "Channel Havens" by Ken Endean has less information but it is neatly presented. On the West Coast of England and Wales I used the "Lundy and Irish Sea Pilot" by Imray which was rather out of date but still worth having. The Clyde Cruising Club produce some excellent pilot books and I selected the "Firth of Clyde" and "Kintyre and Ardnamurchan". On the East Coast I used a Royal Forth pilot book and then a Royal Northumberland one. Perhaps my favourite British pilot book is the "East Coast Pilot" which has excellent advice and informative pictures from Lowestoft to Ramsgate.

I used Admiralty, Stanford and Imray charts. I found that the Imray charts were just about sufficient though sometimes they do not have information on a small harbour you want to visit and you are then dependent on the almanac, which may also be limited. When expecting to anchor, I used an Admiralty chart. The leisure series for the Hebrides was a joy to use and there is real detail to pick out most of the dangers. Admiralty do a specific chart just for Strangford Lough and this was an absolute essential for the Lough.

In my diary and logbook I recorded engine hours and distance travelled. I generally noted the weather and the main events along the way. It helped to make sense of life as well as being a record to be referred to later.

I carried the "Handbook of Sailing" by Bob Bond and the "New

Complete Sailing Manual" by Steve Sleight, which are both superb, clear and comprehensive. I have never been able to fault or improve on the techniques they explain. I carried RYA manuals that I had gathered during courses, including a sea survival manual and a diesel manual. Previous owners had passed on comprehensive manuals about the sails and rigging of Kippa. I also kept photocopies of the manuals for the handheld radio, liferaft, chartplotter, Navtex, GPS, tillerpilot and Yeoman plotter on the boat. I also kept copies of maintenance, contacts, servicing, insurance and licence files, leaving most originals at home.

Appendix G
Clothes and bedding

Clothes I carried were:

4 pairs gloves, two without finger covering
2 hats
2 caps
2 pairs of deck shoes
1 pair of boots
2 breathable vests

3 other vests
5 pants
5 socks
3 trousers
3 shirts
2 large jerseys
1 short-sleeved jersey

I normally wore deck shoes but in bad weather the boots were excellent. The breathable vests were a bit scratchy when you put them on but they certainly worked very well, wicking the sweat away and keeping the body at a nice temperature.

I used a French set of over-trousers and jacket that were super. The cord of the hood broke early on but otherwise they did their job well.

I had lots of gloves and hats so that there were spares for crew who had forgotten these items.

I took a duvet and a sheet and some of the year I used this rather than the sleeping bag. However, during the "summer" I used the sleeping bag and the duvet. I also took two pillows, two cushions and two hot-water bottles (again, spares for crew). There is nothing like climbing into a warm sleeping bag at the end of a tiring day.

My toy dog, Scruff, was aboard the whole journey. Most yachts seem to carry a small stuffed toy, especially when the skipper is solo. Scruff was given to me by Sarah and he would often have something to say about the weather or the sea state was never averse to telling me how tired I looked. He is inclined to be a trifle monosyllabic, though perhaps it is understandable as his whole life has been rough. Rough, rough.

Appendix H
Ports of call

Kippa and I visited the following harbours and anchorages:

Starcross (River Exe)
Teignmouth
Brixham
Dartmouth
Dittisham
Salcombe
Kingsbridge
Newton Ferrers
Saltash
River Tamar
Plymouth
Dandy Hole (St Germans)
Torpoint
Cremyll
Fowey
River Lerryn
Falmouth
Mylor
Pandora Inn
Truro
Malpas
Penryn
Penzance
St Ives
Padstow
Clovelly

Bideford
Croyde Bay
Swansea
Port Eynon Bay
Tenby
Milford Haven
Cleddau Estuary (Llanion)
Solva
Cardigan
New Quay
Aberdovey
Pwllheli
Menai Strait (Port Dinorwic)
Port St Mary (Isle of Man)
Strangford Lough
    (Northern Ireland)
Portaferry
Quoile
Ringhaddy
Strangford
Donaghadee
Portpatrick
Girvan
Troon
Millport (Cumbrae)
Rothesay (Bute)

West Kyle
Portavadie (Loch Fyne)
Ardrishaig
Lochgilphead
Crinan
Ardinamir Bay by the islands
   of Torsay and Luing
Puilldobhran
Kerrera, Oban
Loch Aline
Sanna Bay
Arisaig
The Small Isles of Eigg
   and Muck
Oronsay in Loch Sunart
The Sound of Mull
Loch Creran
Ballachulish (Glencoe)
Loch Linnhe
Onich
Corpach (Fort William)
Laggan (Caledonian Canal)
Fort Augustus
Inverness
Cromarty
Lossiemouth
Portknockie
Whitehills
Macduff
Gardenstown
Rosehearty
Peterhead
Stonehaven
Johnshaven
Arbroath
Anstruther

Elie
Edinburgh (Granton)
Inchcolm
Isle of May
Dunbar
Eyemouth
Lindisfarne
Amble
Blyth
Sunderland
Hartlepool
Whitby
Scarborough
Grimsby
Spurn Head
Wells-Next-The-Sea
Great Yarmouth
Lowestoft
Aldeburgh
Snape
Orford
Butley River
Shotley
Mistley
Ramsgate
Dover
Rye
Eastbourne
Brighton
Littlehampton
Gosport
Poole
Weymouth
Bridport
Exmouth
Topsham

Appendix I
Choosing the boat

Corribee or Hallberg Rassy? £2,500 or £50,000?

I did not start with a budget. Instead I began by working out a set of criteria. I suppose it began with, what is capable of the trip? In fact, a Wayfarer dinghy is capable of the trip. Or smaller than that. But if I was going to live onboard I wanted a cabin. An early decision was to try and find a boat with sufficient headroom. I was advised against limiting my options in that way during my search but, having undertaken the trip, I now know that headroom does matter a lot. I like to be able to cook a reasonable meal aboard and that requires standing up for a while.

The next big decision concerned the keel. The fin keel seemed the least likely option from the outset. A fin can give you good sailing performance but you always need water to float it unless you are going to risk perching it on the fin against a sea-wall.

A long keel appealed because I had experienced the stability and seaworthiness of a long keel. Again it normally needs water to remain upright but it is perhaps a little easier than a fin to lean against a harbour wall. During my search a Nicholson 26 came up to which I gave serious consideration. They are strong, good in a sea and perform well in a strong wind. On the other hand, it has a dated interior and the one I saw needed a lot of work to suit the purpose even though it was a sound little cruiser, as demonstrated by friends of the former owner who kindly took me for a sail in Salcombe Harbour.

A lifting keel, perhaps? I had tried a Southerly 100 lift keel with the children and Keith. It had not really been a satisfying cruiser. It sailed poorly and somehow the lifting up and down was a chore. I also heard horror stories of stones and other objects getting stuck in the keel sheath and causing the keel to jam up or down, potentially tricky either way. I also got the sense that a lift keel can never quite have the sailing performance of a fin. I later heard comments that the keel can slam in its case in certain seas, which must be rather unpleasant.

I looked at bilge keel options – two and three keels. In the end a twin keel appealed most, being capable of reasonable sailing ability while also being ideal for "taking the ground". They sit pretty horizontal, unless you have got it badly wrong, as I did at Rye, normally allowing a good night's sleep because for some hours you can be as if on dry land and really get a rest. There is not much to go wrong with a twin keel and an additional advantage is that if you do touch bottom while sailing, potential disasters are likely to be more survivable. I have also heard it said that your hull has twice the protection if you think of your fins as being your first point of contact with an object.

In terms of makes, I liked the idea of an old Swedish boat, having seen how well built they are. However, they were just too expensive. I did not start out with any prejudice about modern boats, because even Bavaria and Jeanneau have made tough boats in their early days, before mass production, when they established a reputation on solid construction. Beneteaus and Dufours sail well, but somehow they did not give that sense of being suited to the task.

British boats seemed to be designed for British waters. The Westerly has a very active association and a loyal following, so I looked closely at their boats. However the affordable ones were old-fashioned and the later ones too big. A Fulmar comes close, but is expensive. A Konsort nearly did it for me except that the headroom was lacking and, at around £30,000, I was not prepared to pay that much for banging my head. I also learnt that Westerly keels are not as resilient as I imagined.

The name Hunter put me off when I was told that the original owner and builder was a bloodsports enthusiast, so it dropped off my list for quite a while.

I considered a Morecombe Nobby, a wooden boat with a gaff rig. "More romance than practicality" was my conclusion, though I never actually sailed one, despite a kind owner who has several gaff boats offering me a sail in Holland which I could not attend because of work pressure.

A Jeanneau Fantasia 27 caught my fancy at Gillingham because of its super layout and smart design. It has two deep twin keels to give good sailing performance, as well as the ability to dry out. However, I was steered away by a naval architect who told me about keels breaking off Jeanneaus. When I investigated, it appeared repairs to the Fantasia keels were not unheard of. The web also revealed comments about the thickness of the hull that worried me.

Returning to Hunters, I saw that the Horizon 26 and 27 models have a similar layout to the Fantasia with no forecabin so that the saloon feels big and allows space for a largish aft cabin and a heads (sea toilet) in a convenient place. The 272 and 273 are virtually the same and just a bit better on certain details than the 26.

After headroom, keel and sailing performance, the next consideration was the galley. I wanted a grill and oven and the Hunter provided this too. The galley area is limited, as it is on all small yachts, but the cooker is very well designed and it did me proud. I could put together a reasonable meat-and-two-veg meal. A good breakfast was always easy too.

My next decision concerned the engine. Inboard or outboard? I am so pleased I chose the inboard diesel, even though mine packed up and had to be replaced at considerable cost. On a round-Britain cruise I had to resort to the engine. I do not like doing so, I like sailing not motoring, but the reality is that if you are going to get past the next tidal gate and into the next harbour you often have to crack on. For those people happy to drop anchor for six hours when the wind droops, there is no need for an inboard, for example the folkboat is a great design, but you need to be a hardy soul who does not mind bobbing about for hours in nasty conditions. My nerves would not have coped with that and the inboard kept the dream alive and got me out of trouble.

Diesel wins over petrol in most marine applications and the Yanmar 1GM10 is generally very reliable.

I found the Hunter Association members helpful and was soon able to identify several 272 and 273 models that might fit the bill, a very good one in Anglesey and a nice one in Hull, both with amenable owners. A rather tired one on the South Coast I avoided but a good one at Dover was tempting. The owner kept it very spick-and-span but it was a touch limited on equipment and did not feel quite right for me.

Another good one at Beaulieu came on and off the market and then I found Kippa. The very helpful owners were able to answer all my questions and they kindly took me for a sail from Starcross to Teignmouth. Halfway across we more or less shook on the deal! I was sold on Kippa as much because of the owners as anything else. They were practical, neat and well organised people who both knew how to sail competently. They treated the boat with great care and everything was in apple pie order. After-sales turned out to be more than one could ever ask for or expect. They were extremely kind and generous with their time to ensure that I was happy. Indeed, as soon as I sailed her, I was delighted with Kippa and knew right away that I had made the right choice. It was a great feeling after such a long search.

Kippa exceeded expectations in some ways. She handles any sea. She is tough, easy to sail and has no real faults. She is not quick but she is not slow either and can give an exhilarating sail. She is fair rather than spectacular sailing upwind and I would fit a genoa instead of the jib to give her better performance in light airs. I used a scooper sail for light winds, which works brilliantly but is not suited to single-handed sailing. The self tacking jib is fine and I had no problems with it, but for long passages where you are on one tack for several hours, then a genoa would suit me, though for estuary and river sailing and short weekend hops the self-tacking jib is great. I had expected the sliding car to stick and jam but it rarely did. A drop of light grease about three times in the year sorted it.